SCOTTISH MURDERS

compiled by
LISA WALLIS AND
DEREK WRIGHT

LOMOND BOOKS
Broxburn

This edition published by Lomond Books Ltd
Broxburn EH52 5NF, Scotland 2022
www.lomondbooks.com

ISBN 978 1 84204 252 6

Text © Wordsworth Editions Limited 2011

Typeset in Great Britain by Roperford Editorial
Printed and bound in Great Britain by Clays Ltd, Elcograf S.p.A.

SCOTTISH MURDERS

CONTENTS

DAVID RIZZIO AND
MARY QUEEN OF SCOTS

Date: 1566
Location: Edinburgh

DAVID RIZZIO AND
MARY QUEEN OF SCOTS

At the end of Edinburgh's Royal Mile stands the Palace of Holyroodhouse. Now known primarily as the official Scottish residence of the British monarchy, it has been the home of royalty for over five hundred years.

A tour of the palace will take the visitor through opulent state apartments, sumptuously decorated with tapestries and adorned with the finest paintings. But towards the end of the tour there is a perceptible feeling of going back in time as your steps take you into much smaller, plainer rooms – for these are the chambers once occupied by Mary, Queen of Scots. A small spiral staircase takes you to Mary's bedchamber, and there on the floor is a small brass plaque which marks the place where, on the night of 9 March 1566, a man called David Rizzio was murdered. It was an event that marked the start of a downward spiral of intrigue, jealousy and violence that would lead to the death of a queen.

Let us go back to the year 1560, and the day on which the galley carrying Mary from France dropped anchor at the port of Leith. The eighteen-year-old Mary was returning to Scotland for the first time in twelve years. She was the daughter of King James V of Scotland and Mary of Guise, who came from a wealthy and influential French family. After the death of her father, Mary was crowned Queen of Scots at only nine months old. Scotland was to be ruled by a Regent until Mary became of sufficient age to rule, but she was seen immediately by the English king, Henry VIII, as the ideal solution to his plan to gain control of the Scottish throne. Mary of Guise, her staunchly Catholic mother, wished to ensure there was no possibility of her daughter being betrothed in marriage to an English Protestant prince, and despatched her five-year-old daughter to be raised at the French court.

So it was that Mary returned to claim her crown. Despite her young age, Mary was already a widow. At the age of fifteen she had married Francis, the French Dauphin, who became King of France in 1559, but died the year after. Mary, tall, beautiful and well educated, had what many believed was a valid claim to the throne of England, and to Henry VIII's daughter, Elizabeth, now Queen of England, she represented a serious threat.

Not surprisingly, the matter of who would become Mary's next husband became the source of much debate and intrigue. Elizabeth sought to neutralise the threat that Mary posed by marrying her off to Robert Dudley, a nobleman and court favourite, but Mary had other ideas, and in 1565 married Lord Henry Darnley, a man of impeccable pedigree and dazzling good looks. It soon became apparent to Mary that his charms were purely visual. Royal blood may have run through his veins, but during most of his waking hours it was laced with considerable amounts of alcohol. With little innate intelligence, and permanently befuddled wits, he performed no useful function in the governing of Scotland, invariably being absent 'hunting, hawking or whoring'.

With her husband usually absent or comatose, Mary relied on her own court circle for entertainment and companionship, and one of her favourites was David Rizzio. Rizzio was an Italian courtier, the son of a Turin music teacher. Not a particularly attractive man – short, swarthy and rumoured to be hunch-backed – it was his abilities as a musician and a singer that first gained him admittance to court, and entertaining conversation and a pleasing manner made him enjoyable company for Mary. He established himself in the post of her private secretary, and she became increasingly reliant on him. He, for his part, began to exploit his position of influence. Because he had practically unlimited access to the queen at any time, he was able manoeuvre himself into a position where he effectively controlled access to her, showing himself to be not averse to accepting a little bribery from those seeking an audience.

There was a considerable body of opposition to Mary as queen. Scotland was a largely Protestant country, and although Mary was careful to fulfil the ceremonial religious requirements of her position, she did not seek to conceal the fact that, in her private devotions, she remained staunchly Catholic, and there was always an undercurrent of belief amongst the Protestant nobility that she would seek to restore Catholicism as the official religion of Scotland.

The elements of opposition perceived the possibility of using Lord Darnley as a means of undermining the queen. Although pregnant with his child, their infrequent meetings were largely when he would arrive at Holyrood Palace in an advanced state of inebriation, and her resulting hostility towards him made him bitter and resentful. Furthermore, although not having the wit or application to carry out any useful function, it rankled with him that his status as King of Scotland was in name only, the position carrying little dignity, responsibility or power.

As a result, he was open to the poisonous whispers in his ear, which even his addled wits could grasp – that the Queen had been turned against him by the loathsome Rizzio, they said – a lecherous hunchback who had become her lover, they said. Ejected from the Queen's bed, and starved of power thanks to the schemings of this Italian dwarf – what are you going to do about it? – they said.

So it was, on the night of 7 March 1566, that Lord Darnley climbed the spiral staircase into the queen's chambers where she was dining with Rizzio, she at one end of the table, Rizzio at the other. Darnley had drawn up a chair next to the queen, when another figure appeared from the staircase. It was Lord Ruthven, one of the most powerful Protestant lords, and the fact that he was dressed in full armour suggested the visit was not a social one.

Ruthven politely requested the queen that Rizzio should accompany him, and on being asked why, replied that he had committed 'great offence'. Mary demanded from her husband what part he was playing in this apparent conspiracy, but he gave no reply, and she angrily dismissed Ruthven, threatening to have him arrested as a traitor. He made no move to leave, and when Darnley seized the queen, Rizzio realised his danger, and, drawing his dagger, hurriedly moved behind the queen, clutching her skirts. Suddenly, the main door was thrown open and the other Protestant lords involved in the conspiracy entered. Some accounts say that a pistol was held to Mary's heavily pregnant stomach, but, in any event, she was powerless to save her favourite. Rizzio was dragged screaming across the room to the top of the stairs, where the first dagger thrust into his body was made. In a frenzy of violence he was stabbed repeatedly by the conspirators, and his bloody, lifeless body thrown down the stairs. When his corpse was examined later, he was found to have some fifty-seven separate wounds. Later he was given a pauper's burial in Holyrood cemetery.

If the conspirators expected Mary to succumb meekly to their demands, they were in for a surprise. When Darnley returned early the following morning, perhaps sober for once, and feeling considerable guilt, she was able to convince him that he, too, was in danger, for was not the attack an indication that both they and their unborn child were under threat by forces that wished to see her removed from the throne? Later that day, she met with the conspirators, and calmly assured them she was prepared to overlook the unfortunate events of the previous day, and to grant them pardons. In fact, she had already planned with her courtiers to escape to safety, with Darnley, at midnight.

The plan went smoothly, and she was soon safe within the walls of Dunbar Castle, where she wasted no time in gathering together her supporters from within the Scottish nobility. Nine days after Rizzio's murder, she returned to Edinburgh at the head of 8,000 soldiers, but the conspirators were long gone; once they heard that Darnley had disowned them, they realised their cause was doomed.

Secure on her throne once more, the conspiracy broken up, apparently reconciled with her husband, and with the birth of their first child imminent, it seemed that Mary's turbulent life might have reached a period of stability. But it was to be short-lived.

Mary could never forgive Darnley for his part in Rizzio's death, and he had quickly returned to his usual diversions of hard liquor and loose women. She made out a will leaving all of her significant assets to their child, and pondered aloud on the possibility of having her marriage to Darnley annulled on the grounds of his many well-documented transgressions. Darnley was about to find out, like Thomas Becket some four hundred years previously, that monarchs thinking aloud can have unfortunate consequences.

On 19 June 1566, after a difficult birth, Mary bore a son, the new heir to the throne. Ultimately he would become James VI of Scotland and James I of England, uniting the thrones at last.

With her legacy secured, Mary could once more consider the problem of Lord Darnley. Foremost among Mary's supporters was the Earl of Bothwell. Rich, sophisticated (he spoke good French) and gallant, he assumed the role of her protector, and began to consider how he might best resolve her problem. It is difficult to assess how much Mary was involved in the process, but the conspirators who murdered Rizzio, who had been left to sweat for an extended period, were approached with a proposition; their previous misdemeanours would be overlooked if they carried out one last murder . . .

Early in 1567 Lord Darnley had fallen ill, and returned to his family home in Glasgow. When he returned to Edinburgh, he was anxious to return to Holyrood Palace, but as the nature of his ailment was perhaps smallpox, or more likely, syphilis, Mary wanted him kept well away from their son. However, her attitude to him apparently thawed a little, as subsequently she installed him in comfortable style at a house in Kirk o'Fields, just outside Edinburgh, and would spend the evenings at his bedside reading to him and playing cards, and would sometimes spend the night there, although sleeping safely on a different floor.

On the evening of 9 February 1567, she paid her usual visit, but had to leave early, as she was attending a masque being held at the palace to celebrate the marriage of one of her most trusted servants. At about two o'clock the following morning, the whole of Edinburgh was rocked by an immense explosion, and the house at Kirk o'Fields was found to have been reduced to a pile of rubble. A search through the ruins revealed no sign of Lord Darnley, until his body was found, dressed only in a night-shirt, in a nearby garden. There was no sign on the body of any effects of the blast – the cause of death was strangulation. It seems that he had heard some noises in the garden outside the house, and had been lowered down from a window on a chair to investigate. Proceeding through the garden in his nightshirt, he stumbled across the conspirators, who, having despatched him quickly by a method rather less spectacular than they had expected, promptly lit the fuse.

Mary's reaction to Darnley's murder was the complete opposite to how she had reacted to Rizzio's death. This

time, either through genuine grief, or guilt at her involvement, she was devastated; moving between exhaustion and
hysterics, and subject to bouts of ill-health, she found herself becoming ever more reliant on Bothwell's support, and
began to lavish gifts upon him. This proved to be a fatal error.
It was widely suspected that Bothwell was responsible for
Darnley's murder, and it had been noted how little effort
appeared to be being made to track down his killers. It was
left to Darnley's father, the Earl of Lennox, to accuse Bothwell of the murder, and to bring him before an enquiry.
The result was never in doubt – Lennox feared for his safety
too much to attend the trial, and the presence of a large
contingent of Bothwell's armed supporters on hand ensured
the 'Not Guilty' verdict.

At a meeting of the Scottish nobles in Ainslie, Bothwell
proposed that, for the benefit of the country, the queen
should remarry, and selflessly offered himself for the job. The
minor inconvenience of the fact that he was already married
was soon overcome when his wife, not wishing to stand in the
way of his ambition, agreed to a swift divorce on the basis of his
infidelity with a servant girl, so his way was clear. It just
remained to obtain Mary's agreement.

Bothwell's method of achieving this was a little unorthodox.
As Mary's court was making the journey from Stirling to Edinburgh, Bothwell lay in wait with 800 of his men. Declaring that
danger awaited her in Edinburgh, he rode off with her to
the 'safety' of Dunbar Castle, leaving her bewildered court
behind. Having abducted her, Bothwell sealed the arrangement
by taking her – either forcibly or with her consent – to bed.

Whatever the circumstances, Mary subsequently announced
she had forgiven him for abducting her, and that they planned
to wed. Their request to have Protestant banns read for the
marriage were refused, but finally they were wed on 15 May
1567 in the Great Hall at the Palace of Holyroodhouse.

The marriage marked the point of no return in the fortunes of Mary, Queen of Scots. Suspicion of her involvement in the murder of her husband could have been allayed if she had pursued the wrongdoers vigorously. In practice, she had married the prime suspect. The inevitable rebellion was not long in coming. Just a month after their marriage, Mary and Bothwell's army faced their opponents at Carbery Hill. The rebels' cause was made clear by their banner – against a white background, a green tree under which the body of the murdered king lay. Next to the body was his son, James, and the motto 'Judge and avenge my cause, O Lord'.

Substantially outnumbered, Bothwell's troops started to melt away into the woods. Bothwell himself galloped off, ostensibly to get reinforcements from Dunbar Castle. In fact, he just kept riding; Mary never saw him again and he died many years later in a Danish prison.

Mary's reign as Queen of the Scots was over at the age of twenty-five. She was forced to abdicate in favour of her son, James, and her Protestant half-brother, the Earl of Moray was named as regent. Imprisoned in a castle in Lochleven, she made one last bid to gain power, escaping, and raising an army that suffered an ignominious defeat at Langside, near Glasgow. To evade capture, she fled. She could have chosen France, still surely a safe haven for her, but instead she chose England, perhaps in the belief that her cousin, Queen Elizabeth, would surely assist in restoring her to the throne that should be hers. She could not have been more wrong. The Scottish regent was Protestant, Mary unashamedly Catholic, and with Elizabeth unmarried and childless, Mary's credentials as heir to the English throne would make her a constant threat as the focus of any plot against the English throne.

In October 1568, a commission of enquiry was set up to consider Mary's situation. The Scottish regent, the Earl of Moray, presented a casket of letters, allegedly written by Mary to Bothwell urging him to kill Darnley. Mary refused to accept the jurisdiction of an English court over her, but it made no practical difference, because, to all intents and purposes, she was a prisoner, and so she remained for the next eighteen years. The events of those long years of plotting and intrigue do not form part of our story. Mary remained a constant thorn in Elizabeth's side, but Elizabeth could not bring herself to do anything about it, until, in 1586, her secretary of state, Francis Walsingham, decided to make up her mind for her.

Without warning, Mary and her household were transferred to Chartley Hall, near Stafford, and subjected to a far stricter routine by her new jailer. Then Mary had a pleasant surprise – it seemed that her supporters had established a means by which she could smuggle letters in and out in barrels of beer, to her supporters in France, and her strongest ally in England, a wealthy merchant called Anthony Babington. Correspondence began to flow; Babington told of his plan to murder Elizabeth, to free Mary and to seize power, and she responded, giving encouragement. Little did she know that the line of communication was all the work of Francis Walsingham. Every message was intercepted and decoded, the weight of evidence against her building day by day.

On 11 August 1586, Mary was allowed by her jailer to go for a ride, and as she did, she saw a group of riders approaching her – surely Babington's plan had come to fruition, and she was about to be freed? But the riders brought a warrant for her arrest; Babington and his associates had been arrested and tortured, and confessed everything. A search of Mary's rooms revealed a huge stash of letters and cyphers.

Her trial commenced in October in the great hall at Fotheringhay in Northamptonshire. She defended herself bravely, so much so that the trial was adjourned, and resumed in London without her, but the outcome was never in doubt. Found guilty, it fell upon Queen Elizabeth to sign the death warrant.

For three long months she put off the decision, before finally doing so on 1 February 1587.

Mary faced her end with nobility; when her executioner sought her forgiveness, she replied 'I forgive you with all my heart, for now I hope you shall make an end to all my troubles.' Mary ascended the scaffold in the Great Hall at Fotheringhay with quiet dignity, and placed her head upon the block. It took the executioner three attempts to sever her head from her body. As he stooped to pick up the head by its auburn locks, he was left holding a wig, as the head, with its cropped grey hair, rolled away.

So it was that Mary Stuart, Queen of Scots, came to the end of the journey that had begun that night in the Palace of Holyroodhouse over twenty years before. Today, as visitors gaze at that small bronze plaque on the floor, the guide will point out the dark stain upon the floor. For the stain is said to be the blood of David Rizzio, which four hundred years of cleaning has been unable to erase.

THE LEGEND OF SAWNEY BEANE

Date: The late 16th century
Place: South Ayrshire

THE LEGEND OF SAWNEY BEANE

The *Newgate Calendar* was a publication that started out as a record of the executions at that famous prison, but grew into a comprehensive collection of accounts of famous crimes. Between 1750 and 1850, its popularity was such that, along with the Bible and Bunyan's *The Pilgrim's Progress*, it was one of the three books found in most homes, and was used as a way of instilling in children a healthy fear of the perils of wrong doing.

It is the *Newgate Calendar* that provides the most common source of information for the story of Sawney Beane and his family, whose gruesome exploits would not seem out of place in a modern day horror film. The story begins during the reign of Queen Elizabeth, when King James sat upon the throne of Scotland. Alexander 'Sawney' Beane was born in a small East Lothian village just outside Edinburgh. His father was an honest labourer and made his living digging ditches and trimming hedges. From an early age, Sawney was lazy and vicious, with blatant disrespect for authority. He was expected to follow in his father's footsteps and while he did make a brief attempt at earning an honest living, his tendency towards idleness and dishonesty ensured that this particular career path was short-lived.

Sawney left home as soon as he was able, taking with him a woman with a similar dishonest disposition. Soon the two were married, and for reasons that are not clear – perhaps to avoid paying for their accommodation – decided to set up home in a set of caves off the Scottish coast in Ayrshire. The Bennane caves were deceptively large, with tunnels extending more than a mile in length into the solid rock. Additionally, there were a number of side tunnels that could be adapted to provide living quarters. In time, this would allow Sawney and his new wife to accommodate a growing family. The caves were embedded deep into the cliff face. At low tide, they had a sandy beach as a foreshore, but several hundred metres across the entrance to the caves and tunnels were flooded at high tide, twice a day. Although this resulted in rather damp living conditions, it helped to deter intruders, allowing Sawney and his wife to live there in secrecy, and remain undetected for many years.

Sawney's lack of skills or desire to work an honest trade prompted his decision to support his wife through the proceeds of crime, and the caves proved to be a perfect cover for their criminal activities. Not far away, there were a number of lonely and narrow roads that connected the surrounding villages, so it was relatively simple for Sawney to lie in wait, before ambushing and robbing unsuspecting travellers. At some point early in his criminal career, it occurred to Sawney that there was a strong possibility that he would be reported and apprehended for these robberies. At this point, his crimes took a more sinister turn, as he took the decision to murder his victims. After all, the dead could not talk, and therefore Sawney could not be implicated. In his twisted mind, he had fallen upon the perfect solution.

When robbing his victims, Sawney's primary goal was money, which enabled him to buy food at the nearby village shops and markets, but he stole any other items he considered could be of potential value. Sawney was shrewd enough to realise that he should not sell any items that could be deemed recognisable or identified as belonging to someone who had since disappeared, so these valuables were stockpiled in the caves.

Soon Sawney realised that the income generated from the robberies simply was not enough to maintain even their relatively modest lifestyle. By now, the Beanes were living as hermits, and were discovering that the people travelling through this relatively wild and deserted area of Scotland generally did not carry much cash on their person. Sawney was hauling in a good amount of valuables, but the vast majority of these could not be sold as Sawney would quickly be heading for the gallows if he was caught.

Sawney and his wife were often hungry, finding themselves short of food and of cash to buy food. Then it occurred to Sawney that if he was already going to the trouble of robbing and killing his victims, then rather than merely leaving his victims on the deserted roads, why not eat them too? From this point, the twisted practice of cannibalism began to play a large part in the Sawney household. After each robbery and murder, Sawney would drag the bodies back to his cave, where he and his wife would disembowel and dismember the dead bodies. Between them, they salted and pickled the flesh, and this was hung in a makeshift larder in the caves. To avoid detection, the bones were not discarded, but stored in another part of the caves.

Cannibalism became their method of survival, and they seemed to thrive upon it, as Mrs Beane began to produce children. The children were brought up in the caves, and survived on the same diet of human flesh as their parents. Their life had settled into a routine, where Sawney would rob travellers and locals, before bringing their bodies back to the cave to provide the family with food.

These disappearances caused great panic among the local people. The murders had caused enough alarm, but the total disappearance of so many people felt far more sinister. Although enormous efforts were made to find those responsible for the disappearances, the Beanes were never discovered;

the caves in which they lived were simply too deep and complex to be adequately searched. It did not occur to the authorities that anyone, never mind the murderer they were seeking, would live in quarters that were flooded twice daily, and it definitely did not occur to anyone that the missing persons were, in fact, being eaten.

Over an extended period of time without discovery – spanning many years – the Beanes grew more and more confident that they would not be caught. Life settled into an unsettling and disturbing pattern: Sawney continued to rob and murder his victims, before dragging them to the cave to feed his family, and Mrs Beane had a great number of children – all of whom were brought up in the caves.

It seems very unlikely that the children were confined to the caves, and probably spent a great deal of time outdoors at low tide. Their active lifestyle enabled them to exercise; this, coupled with their high protein diet of human flesh, meant that they were all very physically fit and strong. With their food problem solved, the Beanes found they needed to spend very little of the money stolen on food. They used the stolen cash to buy clothing, shoes and other supplies, and often ventured into nearby villages to purchase essentials, blending in with the locals, and attracting no undue attention.

Due, possibly, to having little else to do, Sawney Beane and his wife produced fourteen children. All the children were brought up with the understanding that it was normal practice for them to eat human flesh, and that robbery and murder was merely a job. These fourteen children went on to produce eight grandsons and fourteen granddaughters, all produced by incest. As they grew into adults they were encouraged to participate in the abductions and killing. Over the course of two decades, the Beanes became a self-contained army of killers, murdering and devouring their victims. It was not usual for the Beane men to ambush up to half a dozen people in one single attack, although they were always careful to ensure that they selected only groups that could be easily overpowered. Following the kill, the bodies would be taken back to the caves, where the womenfolk would prepare the flesh for storage in the larder.

Despite the huge numbers in the family, occasionally the Beanes found themselves with too much flesh in the family larder, and some was thrown away due to rotting and decay. It was this careless practice that alerted the authorities to the fact that there may have been more to these disappearances than met the eye. It was not unusual for dismembered and unidentifiable limbs to wash up, but the salting and pickling of the flesh was not normal, and suggested something far more sinister could be going on. Over time, the authorities began to build a disturbing picture of what could be happening.

By this point, the Beanes had been living in the caves for more than two decades, and it is estimated that over a thousand people had disappeared during that period.

It does seem strange that nobody appeared to notice the Beanes. With the ever-growing numbers of children being born, and growing into teenagers, it is unlikely that they were not spotted on the foreshore of the caves when the tide was out. It seems more likely that people did see them and attempt to investigate. They may have strayed too close to the caves, where the Beanes, protective of their home turf, attacked and murdered them.

The investigations into the disappearances of the hundreds of people over the last two decades gathered momentum. There was pressure on the authorities to find the parties responsible, and they expanded their search dramatically. The Beanes continued to live and murder undetected, but an unfortunate number of wrongful arrests and subsequent executions were carried out. This mostly impacted upon the local innkeepers, and was generally based on the fact they had seen the missing persons last. This resulted in a number of innkeepers fleeing the area, which became more and more deserted, the villages resembling ghost towns.

Eventually, the Beane clan made a mistake that ultimately resulted in their downfall. One evening, they attacked a man and his wife as they returned on horseback from a nearby fair. The clan split into two groups to attack the pair. One group pulled the woman from her horse, and rapidly murdered and disembowelled her before the other group were able to overpower her husband. The man saw what had happened to his wife, and realising the fate about to befall him, the husband fought back with his sword, while running his horse at his attackers. A number of the Beanes were trampled by the panicked horse, and were quite seriously injured. At the same time, another group of riders, returning from the same fair, appeared on the scene. The Beanes, realising they were at a disadvantage, fled back to the caves, leaving behind the dead body of the woman, and multiple witnesses. The traumatised man was taken to a magistrate to tell his story. The magistrate was horrified, and immediately instructed a message to be sent to the king, notifying him of their findings.

King James was already aware of the multiple disappearances, and, upon hearing the latest developments, took the matter so seriously that he personally appeared in Galloway accompanied by an army of around four hundred men and a vast number of tracker dogs. The area was combed thoroughly as it had been before, but it seemed without result once more. However, as the army was passing by the entrance to the caves the tracker dogs halted them. The dogs had detected a very faint scent of decaying human flesh, and immediately began howling, barking and attempting to drag the soldiers into the dark and damp caves.

The king's men realised that the manhunt had reached its end. They took no chances, and mounted a strategic operation to station men at each and every entrance to the caves, before the remaining armed troops entered and began to systematically search the caves and side tunnels. They eventually found all forty-eight Beanes at the end of the mile-long tunnel. The sights they beheld must have been truly horrific – the cave was full of pieces of dried and cured human flesh hanging from the cave roof, and oak barrels were filled with pickled limbs. All around them were piles and piles of valuables and trinkets stolen from their victims. The notorious Beanes had finally been discovered, but true to form, they did not go quietly, and a brutal and vicious fight ensued. However, the Beanes were hopelessly outnumbered and stood no chance of escape. All were arrested and taken to Edinburgh.

The Beanes did not stand trial. At this time in Scotland, there were certain crimes considered so horrific that the perpetrators were not considered worthy of trial. Their collective crimes were considered so heinous that the Beanes suffered a fate not dissimilar to their victims. The twenty-seven men were all dismembered – their hands and legs were cut off, and they were left to bleed slowly to death while their women watched. When the men were dead, the women were burned to death at the stake.

At no point did any of the Beanes show any remorse for these atrocities, and it is difficult to say whether the younger Beanes truly realised that they had committed any crimes. The unarguably evil Sawney Beane was the head of the clan, and had brought up his children and grandchildren in an isolated and cannibalistic cave-dwelling existence, with Sawney himself dictating their moral and ethical standards – teaching them that murder and cannibalism was normal human behaviour. Regardless of whether they knew right from wrong, they all paid the ultimate penalty.

*   *   *

Is there any truth in the legend of Sawney Beane? There are no contemporary records that confirm it, and details were first published at a time when there was widespread anti-Scottish feeling in England, 'Sawney' being an abusive English nickname for a Scotsman. Equally, there is probably enough evidence to suggest that this, like many legends, contains at least a grain of truth.

BURKE AND HARE

Date: 1827–28
Place: Edinburgh

In the early nineteenth century, medical science was beginning to flourish, and the University of Edinburgh was a renowned institution for medical studies – particularly the study of the anatomy of the human body. At this time, the only cadavers legitimately available for medical studies were those of recently executed criminals, but as the demand for cadavers was increasing drastically, the number of executions being carried out had gone into a sharp decline. This was, in part, down to changes in the penal code – the removal of hanging as a penalty for pick-pocketing in 1808 set the wheels in motion, and over the course of the 1820s and 1830s, the death penalty was removed from a number of other offences.

This decline resulted in only two or three corpses a year being available, which obviously did not meet the ever-growing demand, and over time, resulted in a form of black market for corpses. A number of medical teachers, wanting to protect their teaching reputation, were ready and willing to resort to purchasing bodies when they became available; naturally, grave robbing increased dramatically. As disturbing as this was, the situation soon worsened, and it was not long before some particularly enterprising criminals began what was known at the time as 'anatomical killing'. Put simply, this was targeted killing, ultimately resulting in the victims' cadavers earning a significant amount of money for their killers.

William Burke and William Hare were immigrants from Ulster, originally arriving in Edinburgh as labourers to work on the New Union Canal. The pair worked together for some time, and eventually Burke and his partner, Helen McDougal, moved from Leith into a boarding house run by Hare and his partner, Margaret Laird. Margaret Laird's late husband originally owned Log's Lodgings in Tanner's Close, and while not married, Hare and Laird lived together, and were generally assumed to be husband and wife, she calling herself Mrs Hare.

Burke and Hare became firm friends, and with a mutual greed and disregard for honest labour, were keen to identify other, easier, opportunities to make money.

Such an opportunity soon presented itself when a fellow tenant in Tanner's Close died unexpectedly. The man, known only as Donald, was an elderly army pensioner. At the time of his death, he owed Hare £4 in rent. Hare, being aware of the demand for dead bodies in the medical profession, saw an opportunity to regain his money with minimal effort. On the day of the old man's funeral, Burke and Hare filled the coffin with a bag of bark, and brought the body to the university in the hope of finding a buyer. After making some discreet enquiries, they were directed to a Dr Robert Knox by one of his students. Knox was a highly ambitious anatomist, and eagerly accepted the cadaver. Burke and Hare were paid £7 10s for their trouble – significantly more than the pensioner's initial debt.

Burke and Hare celebrated their easily-gained cash, but the money soon ran out, and once again they were seeking an opportunity to earn more. When another of Burke's tenants fell ill, though by no means seriously, they took it upon themselves to relieve his suffering. The victim, known as Joseph the Miller, was plied with whisky – perhaps offered by Burke for medicinal purposes. When Joseph was significantly under the influence, Burke and Hare overpowered and killed him. Their preferred method of murder was to stop the victim breathing by covering his nose and mouth, whilst the other

restrained him. This ensured the victim sustained no suspicious markings during death, so that the university received
fresh and undamaged cadavers – a significant improvement
when compared to some of the corpses that were supplied by
grave robbers. Eventually, this method of murder became
known as 'Burking'.

Soon, the money ran out once more. By this point, Burke
and Hare had become tired of trying to earn an honest living,
and with no more sickly tenants available, were forced to
consider alternative options. They decided the best course
of action was to lure victims off the street, and in February
1828, they invited a pensioner, Abigail Simpson, to spend
an evening with them before returning to her own home.
Once again, they adopted what was to become their standard
method of murder, and plied her with alcohol. When she
became intoxicated, they overpowered and smothered her;
they returned to the university, where Dr Robert Knox was
once again more than happy to take the body off their hands.
This time, they were paid £10.

By now, Burke's partner Helen McDougal was questioning
where the money was coming from, seeing no evidence of her
partner working a regular job. Deciding she could be trusted,
they had told her the method of their ill-gotten earnings, and
having been enlightened as to the source of their cash, Helen
began to play her own part in their evil scheme. The next
time, Helen befriended a woman, and invited her into the
boarding house for a drink. The two women chatted and
drank together, although Helen was careful to ensure that her
companion drank significantly more, and the woman soon
became intoxicated. Helen then sent for the victim's husband,
telling him his wife was intoxicated and required escorting
home. The husband duly arrived at the inn to take her home.
Burke and Hare, having killed the woman already, then overpowered the husband and murdered him too.

Initially, Burke and Hare chose their victims carefully, preferring those who were not easily recognisable, or those whose
disappearance was unlikely to arouse suspicion, such as visitors
to the town. They also took great care to ensure that they
could not be tied to the boarding house in any way, often
inviting strangers back to the inn. When their disappearance
was reported, neither Burke nor Hare would be linked to
them. Their next victims were two young women, Janet Brown
and Mary Patterson, whom Burke had first encountered in
Canongate, Edinburgh. Mary Patterson was a teenage prostitute, and, mentioning he owned a boarding house, Burke
lured the two women back with him. In his usual style, Burke
plied them with drink, and Mary soon passed out. However,
Janet remained conscious and left the house, saying she would
return later for Mary. On her return, Mary was nowhere to
be found, and she was told that Mary had left with Burke
some time earlier. Janet insisted on waiting, until her landlady
became concerned and sent a message with a servant telling
Janet to leave immediately. Actually Mary had been lying dead
in the house the whole time, and had Janet become more
intoxicated, she was certain to have suffered the same fate.

According to contemporary accounts, Burke appears to have
played the primary role in luring the victims to the boarding
house, and the scale of his activities increased. The next victim
was again identified by Burke, a local beggar woman known
only as 'Effie'. Burke promptly murdered her, and was paid
£10 for her corpse. He quickly moved on, 'saving' a woman in
trouble with the police by claiming that he knew her; hours
later, she was dead, and her body on Dr Knox's dissection
table. Burke quickly found two more vulnerable victims –
an old woman and her grandson. Their bodies were sold for
£8 to Dr Knox.

As his greed escalated, Burke began to lose control, and
became more and more careless and remorseless. He no longer

stuck to visitors and degenerates: his next two victims were an acquaintance of his, known only as 'Mrs Ostler', and more shockingly, a relative of his partner, Helen McDougal. Although Burke appeared to have no qualms about killing her, on this occasion he did ask that Hare actually carry out the killing. It is not clear whether Helen knew of Burke's plans or the fate of her relative.

Hare was responsible for identifying their next victim. A former tenant of his guest-house, Mary Haldane, found herself upon hard times. Unable to pay her rent, and effectively homeless, she appealed to Hare for permission to sleep in his barn. Hare agreed, and then killed her. Shortly after, the next victim appeared on their doorstep. Mary's daughter, Peggy (also a prostitute), had heard that Mary had last been seen with Hare, and knocked at the door of Log's Lodgings, seeking her mother. Hare claimed he had seen her, but not since the week before. He invited Peggy into the house to talk more, and killed her. Both Mary and Peggy were sold to the university, and earned Burke and Hare £10 apiece.

The Haldane killings indicate the beginning of the downward spiral. Peggy and Mary were well known in the area, and their disappearance did not go unnoticed. At this point, the logical solution for Burke and Hare would have been to lie low and refrain from killing. They had had a decent run, and had made a significant amount of money; had they stopped killing then, they might well have got away with their crimes. However, their greed knew no bounds, and they became even more careless.

Their next victim was a well-known children's entertainer, James Wilson, known affectionately as 'Daft Jamie'. Jamie was well known in the town and was easily identifiable, as he had a significant limp due to a deformed foot. Jamie was eighteen at the time of his murder, but despite his deformity, and being mentally retarded, he was physically very strong. He resisted and it ultimately took both men to overpower and eventually kill him. This time, his body was sold to the university but was immediately recognised by several students in Knox's class, who raised questions as to the circumstances of Jamie's death, and how Knox had come upon his body. Indeed, Jamie was a poor choice of victim; he was survived by his mother, who naturally began asking questions as to the fate of her son. Dr Knox denied to his students that the body belonged to 'Daft Jamie', but, tellingly, began to dissect the face first, and quickly removed the feet.

The next victim proved to be the last. Burke and McDougal had left Log's Lodgings boarding house by now. Burke and Hare had argued over Burke's suspicions that the Hares were selling bodies behind his back. Burke and McDougal, angry, had moved out and acquired their own boarding-house, also taking in lodgers. Marjorie Campbell Docherty was lured into their guest-house when Burke pretended that his mother was a Docherty and managed to convince Marjorie that they were actually related. Burke was prevented from killing her immediately, as he had planned, by two other guests boarding at the time, the Grays. The Grays went out for the evening, and shortly after that, neighbours of Burke reported hearing sounds of a struggle. The Grays returned later that evening, and enquired what had happened to Marjorie. Burke told them that she had been asked to leave after being 'overly friendly' with him, which had upset Helen McDougal. In actual fact, Marjorie was dead and hidden in the spare room, under a layer of straw. Ann Gray became suspicious when she and her husband were sternly warned to keep out of the spare room, despite her protestations that she had left a pair of her stockings in there. When they were left alone for the evening, they investigated the spare room and found the body under the bed.

Horrified, they immediately confronted Helen McDougal, who panicked and offered them £10 a week to remain silent.

The couple refused and left to report Burke and Helen to the police. Somehow Helen must have warned Burke, for by the time the police arrived and checked under the bed, Marjorie's body had disappeared. It had actually made it to Dr Knox's dissection table, and Burke had been paid. Burke and Helen were taken into custody. Under separate questioning regarding Marjorie's alleged departure from their guest-house, Burke stated that she had left at 7 a.m., while Helen claimed it was early evening. The discrepancy in their story led to their arrest. Shortly after, the police received an anonymous tip-off and duly recovered Marjorie's body from the Edinburgh medical school. James Gray subsequently identified the body, and categorically confirmed it was Marjorie. Shortly after this, the Hares, too, were arrested and charged.

An Edinburgh paper published a story on the suspected killers, which included details of a number of the locals who had disappeared. Janet Brown, the prostitute who had narrowly escaped Burke and Hare, heard about this and contacted the police. Mary Patterson's clothing had been discovered during a police search. Janet was able to identify this, and also to identify Burke and Hare as the men who had plied both the girls with alcohol.

Despite the sixteen murders, after a month of questioning, the evidence against Burke and Hare was still only circumstantial. Fearing that they might go free, Lord Advocate Sir William Rae offered Hare immunity from prosecution if he testified against Burke and McDougal. The frightened Hare saw a chance to save himself, and readily agreed.

Burke and McDougal stood trial; both were charged with the murder of Marjorie Docherty, while Burke alone stood trial for the murder of Mary Patterson and James Wilson. Found guilty, Burke was sentenced to death by hanging. The case against Helen McDougal was 'Not Proven', and she walked free.

On 28 January 1829, William Burke was hanged. Over 25,000 people arrived to cheer the event in the Lawnmarket. In an ironic twist, Burke's body was donated to the medical school for what was known as 'useful dissection'. His skeleton can still be found in the Surgical School, along with his death mask.

There was much public outcry that James Hare was permitted to walk free, but despite efforts from Daft Jamie's mother to bring him to justice, he was released in February 1829. According to rumours, he escaped to London via a postal coach, but his identity was subsequently discovered and he was thrown into a pit of lime by an angry mob. He is reported to have ended his days as a penniless blind beggar living on the London streets.

Despite his part in the murders, and the significant evidence that he gave 'probable cause' for the murders, Dr Knox escaped prosecution. However, his reputation was so significantly damaged, that he eventually fled Edinburgh and moved to London.

Students participating in the dissection of Burke's body made a pocketbook of his skin. This is engraved in gold with 'Burke's skin 1829' and is displayed to this day in the police museum on the Royal Mile.

A DREAM OF MURDER

Date: 1830
Place: Assynt

A DREAM OF MURDER

The parish of Assynt in the north-west highlands of Scotland is famous for its landscapes and spectacular mountains, a wild, remote and beautiful area much loved by hikers and climbers. But it was here, in 1830, that a murder was committed, and solved apparently by supernatural means.

It was in April of that year that a young farm servant, John Mackenzie, was walking by Loch Tor-na-Eigin, a remote mountain lake about a mile from the village of Drumbeg. As he passed, he noticed a dark shape in the shallow water at the edge of the lake, and on moving closer, he realised it was the body of a man. After dragging the corpse ashore, he could see that the man had come to a violent end, as there was extensive damage to the head. The man's pockets were empty, having been pulled inside out, and there were no signs of a backpack, or any other possessions. Mackenzie went to find help, and soon there were about fifty people from surrounding farms congregated by the lake. Two of them, a young local schoolmaster called Hugh Macleod and a younger boy, Donald Graham, were despatched to undertake the six-mile walk to the manse to notify the local minister of the death.

The victim had been identified by one of the men present as Murdoch Grant, a twenty-five-year-old itinerant English pedlar. The pedlar was a common sight for the time, and for remote areas of the countryside, he represented the sole source of many items, some luxury, some more essential, that could be otherwise difficult to obtain without undertaking a lengthy journey to a larger town. Some pedlars specialised in pots and pans and other practical items, but Grant's wares were more tempting – a fine selection of good quality stockings, handkerchiefs and other material. Although based in Strathbeg, Grant's regular circuit took him through Sutherland, Ross and Cromarty. Life on the road could be a hazardous business because, apart from the value of the goods he carried, as he continued on his circuit and sold his wares, the amount of money in his possession steadily increased.

Grant had travelled to Assynt to attend the wedding of a local girl, Betty Fraser, on 11 March. He was known to have set out with about £5 in cash and about £50 of goods for sale, but business had been good on his journey, and most of his wares had been turned into cash. After the wedding, Grant was offered accommodation by his regular customers in the area, so he stayed on for a few days before setting out on the road once more. He was last seen on the road to Nedd, which would lead him home to Strathbeg.

With the light fading fast, and not wishing to move the body from the place of its discovery, the local people decided to return it to the lake for the night, securely moored, and returned early the following day with the minister and a coffin. Grant was buried in a grave by the loch.

By this time news of the death had reached the procurator fiscal, who was not impressed to learn of the hasty interment, given the suspicious circumstances in which the body had been found. Mr Lumsden, the Sheriff of Inverness, was despatched to the scene to disinter the body, and a post-mortem was carried out by two local surgeons on the banks of the loch, with a crowd of local people as spectators. The body was quite well preserved, due to the antiseptic qualities of the moss on the banks of the lake where the body had lain. On examining the head wounds, the surgeons concluded that death was caused by a number of blows, probably inflicted with a hatchet or hammer.

The Sheriff's inquiries were complicated by the fact that many of the local people only spoke Gaelic, so on the recommendation of the minister, the local schoolmaster, Hugh Macleod, was given the job of acting as translator. Macleod was the son of a local farmer; his father had been determined that Hugh should receive a good education and had hired the services of a tutor, as there was no local school in Assynt at that time. Hugh had grown into a well-educated young man, well thought of in the area, and in 1828 he was appointed assistant schoolmaster at a school at Coigarth in Lochbroom.

However, Macleod's respectable exterior concealed a darker side. Apart from a weakness for pretty girls, he liked to dress well, but found that his salary from teaching did not match his expenditure on clothes, so he decided to supplement it a little. He had broken into a shop in Lochbroom and apart from emptying the till, he stole a quantity of tartan, which he concealed for some months before having a suit made from it. Further thefts were carried out in the months that followed.

Mr Lumsden's investigation into the murder made little progress. Without witnesses, or anything approaching a clue as to the perpetrator, there was little more he could do, and it seemed the case was destined to remain unsolved. It was some time later that the Sheriff called in to the local post-office, and, in passing, the postmaster recalled that a short time after the murder, he was asked to change a £10 Bank of England note for someone that he would not expected to have such funds at his disposal – Hugh Macleod, the schoolteacher. On questioning, Macleod denied that such a transaction had taken place, and denied any involvement in the crime, but Mr Lumsden felt he had sufficient grounds to arrest him, and Macleod was committed to Dornoch jail.

But once again, Mr Lumsden found himself frustrated. A search of Macleod's house failed to unearth any evidence linking him to the crime, and his early release from jail seemed inevitable. It was then that the case took an un-expected turn.

Kenneth Fraser was a tailor who worked in Clachtoil. He was acquainted with Macleod, had gone drinking with him for two days in early April, and been surprised by Macleod's insistence on paying for every round. His contribution to the case was rather unusual. Fraser asserted that he had had a dream, in which he had seen the Macleods' cottage, and a voice in Gaelic had said 'The pack of the merchant is lying in a cairn of stones in a hole near their house.'

What the Sheriff's reaction was to this is not recorded, but in the absence of any better option, a search was undertaken and although nothing was found in the exact location described, the search was widened until, under a pile of stones, a backpack and other articles were found and confirmed to be those of the deceased.

There was some doubt expressed over the veracity of Fraser's story. Had he in fact been told the truth by Macleod while they were both inebriated during their drinking session, and only recalled it in a dream – or indeed, was he an accomplice to, or the perpetrator of the foul deed? Shortly after, the case against Macleod was strengthened considerably when a pair of stockings, identified as belonging to the late pedlar, was discovered amongst his possessions at his father's house. So it was, on 27 September 1830, Macleod appeared before Lord Moncrieff at the Circuit Court in Inverness, charged with the murder of Murdoch Grant.

Kenneth Fraser, or 'Kenneth the Dreamer' as he was now known, recounted the story of his dream impressively, and the weight of circumstantial evidence presented by the prosec-ution against Macleod grew steadily. The defence called no witnesses, and the unanimous verdict of 'Guilty' came as no surprise, although Macleod sprung to his feet and exclaimed 'The Lord Almighty knows that I am innocent. I don't think anyone in this country would be condemned by mere opinion.' The judge donned the symbolic black cap, and pronounced that Macleod would hang in Inverness on 24 October, his body to be given to the Professor of Anatomy in Edinburgh for dissection. It was when Macleod was returned to his cell, that he told the true story of the murder of Murdoch Grant.

In his quest to acquire more money, pedlars had become an increasingly tempting target for Macleod, and so he sought to make the acquaintance of Murdoch Grant. Spending some time with him the day before the murder, he arranged to meet Grant the following day, when they would go to Macleod's home in Lynmeanach, as he wished to make a substantial purchase. The following morning, Macleod selected a heavy hammer from the barn at home, donned his father's greatcoat to conceal the weapon, and set off for the road to Nedd to meet Grant at noon as they had arranged.

After they met, they set off over the moorland, and as they approached Loch Tor-na-Eigin, Macleod struck out with the hammer, stunning Grant, then battering him about the head until he was dead. The deed done, he took all the cash from the dead man's pockets, and dragged the body as far as he dare venture out into the loch. The hammer was hurled as far as he could out into the depths. Returning to the shore, he took the heaviest items from the pedlar's pack and sank them in a peat bog, keeping the lighter items to take with him. Concealing the pack near his home, he spent the following weeks clearing his debts, buying new clothes and taking his friends out drinking.

However, each day his journey took him past the loch and its awful secret, and each day he saw the water level gradually sinking, but dared not risk attempting to move the body. Then came the day when a sharp-eyed farm servant passed by . . .

Hugh Macleod went to the scaffold dressed in a long black robe and a white cap, as was the custom in those parts. In the course of a long rambling address to the crowd watching the execution, he cleared 'Kenneth the Dreamer' of any involvement in the crime. As his time on this earth drew to a close, he reflected on what had brought him to such an unhappy end: 'If I were to live for one hundred years, never would I put a glass to my head, never would I hold a card in my hand.'

THE CASE OF
MISS MADELEINE SMITH

Date: 1857
Place: Glasgow

On Thursday, 9 July 1857, a great crowd gathered outside the High Court in Edinburgh. The atmosphere was charged to fever pitch as the crowd waited in anticipation for the verdict of one of the most sensational trials of the 19th century. Hanging in the balance was the fate of Madeleine Hamilton Smith, an attractive young girl from a wealthy Glasgow family, who stood accused of murdering her lover, Emile l'Angelier.

Some months earlier, just past 2 a.m. on 23 March 1857, Emile l'Angelier stumbled through the dark streets of Glasgow, clutching his stomach and groaning in pain. His landlady discovered him at the front door of her lodging house after hearing his groans, and helped him to bed to recuperate. Concerned, she asked him if he had eaten anything that might have caused this illness. Emile claimed not, but his landlady suspected otherwise, this being his third attack of a similar nature in less than two months. Over the course of the night, Emile's condition deteriorated rapidly and the landlady fetched a doctor at around 5 a.m. The doctor prescribed laudanum-laced water to relieve the pain. The doctor visited twice more, once around 7 a.m. and later around 11 a.m. On receiving the doctor for the second visit, the visibly relieved landlady told him that Emile had been sleeping soundly. After examining the 'sleeping' Emile, the doctor instructed the landlady to close the curtains; then he broke the news that the patient was dead.

* * *

Emile l'Angelier was born in the Channel Islands to French
parents, who worked as seed merchants, and ran a small but
successful business out of their modest house. Emile was sent
to Edinburgh to work as an apprentice, and he worked in a
number of nursery jobs over the course of the next decade, in
Edinburgh and France, before ultimately ending up in Glasgow, working in a warehouse. Also living in Glasgow was
Madeleine Smith, the first of five children born to her parents,
James and Elizabeth Smith. James Smith was a wealthy archi-
tect and a prominent member of the upper class. In the 19th
century, class was taken very seriously, and Madeleine was
educated in the traditional style of the time. She accompanied her parents to parties and social occasions, and enjoyed
the comfortable lifestyle afforded to those in the upper
class. In her late teens, Madeleine was sent to London to
attend Mrs Alice Gorton's Academy for Young Ladies. At
the academy, Madeleine was taught the traditional lessons of
the time – manners, piano lessons, crafts – and other skills
deemed appropriate for young ladies. Madeleine returned to
the family home at eighteen, where it was expected she would
adopt the meek and docile role expected from a daughter of
her class. As we will discover, this is not a role that suited
Madeleine's bold temperament.

Madeleine, upon her return from London, attended a great
number of society balls, once managing to attend five in one
night. At some point, Emile noticed her, and, smitten, he
made it his mission to gain an introduction to the attractive
Madeleine. On Valentine's Day in 1855, Madeleine attended
a ball, and received a single red rose from an anonymous
admirer. Perhaps she wondered if this came from the dashing
foreign-looking gentleman whom she would see so often
sauntering up and down Sauchiehall Street. Over several
weeks of encountering Madeleine and her sister without introduction or greeting, he persuaded a friend of his, who

knew Madeleine, to come walking with him on Sauchiehall Street. At the appropriate moment, the friend would introduce l'Angelier to Madeleine. The acquaintance was required to perform the introduction, as it was not socially acceptable for young women to be greeted unannounced by strangers.

L'Angelier's friend readily agreed, and so, Madeleine Hamilton Smith, the beautiful daughter of one of the richest and most prominent families in Glasgow, made the acquaintance of Emile l'Angelier, a modest warehouse worker and ten years her senior. After this initial meeting, Madeleine's sister, Bessie, apparently believed that l'Angelier was interested in her; Madeleine knew this to be wishful thinking, for Bessie, two years her junior, was plainer and plumper.

Madeleine was immediately impressed by this foreigner, who would talk often of his background, frequently mentioning the counts, marquises and dukes of the old French nobility from whom he claimed to be descended. The fact that he was an immigrant earning a mere ten shillings per week from the Bothwell Street seedsmen would only have added to his romantic intrigue and Madeleine was immediately hooked. The pair began to plan opportunities to meet. However, for all his worldly talk, l'Angelier was a traditional type, and made it clear to Madeleine, early in their friendship, that he did not approve of her lifestyle, and the fact she would attend society balls and flirt with young gentlemen. This did not, however, dampen his affection for her, and he soon sent her another red rose.

Madeleine was an astute young woman, immediately realising that a friendship between a lady of her social stature and a working-class man such as Emile was highly inappropriate and would be frowned upon. However, she was very attracted to Emile, and found him a welcome distraction from the monotony and tedium of her normal society life. There may have been an element of rebellion in their friendship, as Madeleine would have been well aware of the reactions of her family, were they to find out. This can only have added to the excitement of their clandestine meetings.

Their bond seemed to develop quickly, and after a short time they were arranging secret meetings on a regular basis. Several times they were bold enough to arrange to meet on the street or in a nearby shop. However, not long after their friendship began, Madeleine's father moved the family out of Glasgow to the nearby town of Rowaleyn. Shortly after the move, in April of 1855, she wrote Emile a brief note that began:

'My Dear Emile, I do not feel as if I were writing you for the first time. [We] have become as familiar friends. May we long continue . . .'

This prompted a rapid flurry of correspondence, and letters flew back and forth between the pair on a regular basis. It is not known how many letters they exchanged over the course of their affair, but nearly two hundred were found in l'Angelier's quarters after his death, and sixty of these were read aloud at her trial. Very few letters from l'Angelier were discovered. It may have been that Madeleine destroyed them for fear of them being discovered by a member of her family. At any rate, Madeleine's second letter to l'Angelier suggested contriving a meeting.

Madeleine's sister Bessie discovered that l'Angelier was in correspondence with her sister, and was, given her own crush on the dashing foreigner, naturally quite jealous. To get her own back, Bessie told her father than Madeleine had been out walking alone with a gentleman not known to him. James Smith was extremely angry with this news, and told Madeleine she was no longer to see the Frenchman. Madeleine told her father that she had been introduced to him by a mutual friend, and had not seen that there should be a problem walking with him, as a mutual friend had introduced them.

Annoyed that Madeleine had got away with this, and that her correspondence with l'Angelier had continued, Bessie tattled once again, this time telling her father that l'Angelier was not only a foreigner, but also a near-penniless labourer. Smith was appalled – l'Angelier was nowhere near appropriate as a suitor for his daughter's hand and it would not do if anyone in their social circle were to learn of this dalliance. Madeleine's mother reacted with great disappointment to Madeleine's choice. Between her father's anger and her mother's tears, Madeleine decided that she would end the affair.

She wrote once more to l'Angelier, a short, polite note wishing him happiness in the future, but confirming that their friendship must end. Only part of the note survives, the remainder either destroyed by l'Angelier or lost over time, but the meaning is clear. But, although the correspondence stopped, the courtship still went on, with l'Angelier, unwilling to accept that the relationship was over, continuing to hang around India Street, where Madeleine lived. When she was able, she would let him into the house via the laundry room.

Emile was hopelessly in love with Madeleine and confided his feelings to an older lady friend of his, Miss Mary Perry. Perry was an old spinster, but a romantic at heart, and she was touched by the plight of the young couple. She suggested to l'Angelier that he bring Madeleine to her house at Renfrew Street when she was able. Emile duly did so, and after meeting Madeleine, Miss Perry kindly offered her home as a place where the couple could meet in secret.

Over time, the couple planned all their assignations here, while Mrs Perry made herself scarce; so the relationship continued, albeit covertly, and without the knowledge of her father for a time. In July, her father found out that they had continued to meet, and laid down the law. This time, he let Madeleine know in no uncertain terms that the relationship was to cease. Madeleine wrote, to l'Angelier and to Miss Perry this time, to confirm that it was over. Again, the attempt to end the affair failed, with Emile refusing to accept that she would no longer see him. A letter from Emile to Madeleine was discovered later, in which Emile tells Madeleine she had deceived not only him, but also her father, and suggesting that he may send her letters to her father for perusal.

The pair began to correspond again, albeit carefully. Emile could not send or deliver letters to the family home, as two attempts had been made recently to burgle the family home and the residence was being carefully watched. Ever resourceful, the pair continued to meet in Miss Perry's home, and letters were written. Emile wrote to Madeleine under the name of 'Miss Bruce' and sent them care of the Post Office. Madeleine's servant Christina Haggerty collected the letters for her.

Over the following months, their relationship became more serious. The Smith family moved once again, to a property in Blythwood Street, which helped Madeleine's problem with the letters. Blythwood Street was just a fifteen-minute walk from Emile's lodgings, and Madeleine's bedroom was in the basement. The windows, while barred, were at street level and a letter could be dropped through. This arrangement also enabled Emile to visit Madeleine's bedroom window from time to time. He was forced to bribe the police officer watching the street with cigars to make this possible, and the policeman turned a blind eye.

They began to plan their wedding, and became lovers – a shocking taboo in Victorian times as sex outside of marriage was not permitted, particularly not between members of differing classes, such as Emile and Madeleine. In their correspondence, they referred to each other as husband and wife, despite not being married or formally engaged. Emile kept every letter Madeleine sent, though Madeleine was ordered to burn his immediately. It is thought this was due to Emile's fear that a member of the Smith family would discover them and put a stop to their romance.

In the meantime, Madeleine's family had been busy planning their daughter's future wedding, and had identified a wealthy and successful suitor. William Minnoch was a merchant who lived near to the Smith family. Minnoch moved in the same social circles as the Smiths, and was very wealthy, with an income of around £3,000 a year. Around this time, Emile's salary increased to £1 a week, a substantial difference for him, but too late for Madeleine, who was growing tired of him and was trying to distance herself from their relationship.

Minnoch courted Madeleine, initially from afar, and it was around this time, in late 1856, that l'Angelier began to question Madeleine about gossip and rumours he had heard regarding her flirtation with others. Madeleine responded to Emile claiming that her love for him remained true, and that l'Angelier was to ignore reports. She told him that he might hear reports that she was to marry, but that these were untrue, and that he must not enter into a dialogue with Minnoch if he were to encounter him, as this would only result in him becoming rude.

Over the summer, the possibility of Emile and Madeleine marrying grew smaller. Minnoch was making regular calls to the Smith family home in the day, while Emile would meet with Madeleine in the gardens at night.

A letter to Emile in late September read:

'Would you leave me to end my days in misery. For I can never be the wife of another, after our intimacy. But, sweet love, I do not regret that – never did, and never shall. Emile, you were not pleased because I would not let you love me last night. Your last visit you said "you would not do it again until we were married".'

In the letters, Madeleine's feelings seemed to be cooling. The declarations of love became less frequent and Minnoch's name was mentioned more and more regularly. James Smith, deciding that Minnoch was an ideal suitor, invited him to join the family for the summer at their holiday home. He spent a great deal of time with Madeleine, who very much enjoyed his company. The fact that Madeleine liked William, as well as recognising that their relationship was far more socially acceptable to her family and society in general, led her to encourage his affections, and she eagerly accepted his proposal which came in January 1857. The Smith family, naturally, were delighted.

This now posed a problem for Madeleine. With her future husband in place, Madeleine had no further need or desire for Emile, and wrote to him shortly after her engagement to declare her feelings toward their marriage. Her letter told Emile that she saw little chance of their marrying, the letter ended:

'If we could only get married all would be well. But alas, alas, I see no chance. No chance of happiness for me.'

Apparently furious, Emile returned the letter; Madeleine, seeing a chance to drive the point home responded:

'I felt truly astonished to have my last letter returned to me. But it will be the last you have the opportunity in returning to me. When you are not pleased with the letters I send you, our correspondence shall be at an end, and as there is coolness on both sides, our engagement had better be broken.'

The letter continues:

'I know you will never injure the character of one you so fondly loved. No, Emile, I know you have honour and are a gentleman. What has passed you will not mention. I know when I ask you, that you will comply.'

She went on to name a time and place where Emile was to meet her servant, Christina Haggarty, where she would collect all Madeleine's letters from him.

Emile was extremely angry at this development, and was anything but compliant. In a rage, he ignored her letter. Shortly after he heard word of her engagement. Upon receiving another of Madeleine's letters, once again requesting her letters back, he refused. He told Madeleine he considered her to be his wife, and, threatening to tell her father of their relationship, he insisted that their relationship continue.

Madeleine wrote twice more, begging Emile not to reveal their relationship and sexual history. Knowing she ran the risk of losing her new fiancé and being thrown out of the family home, Madeleine asked Emile to meet once more. Emile, feeling he had once again gained his own way, agreed.

Madeleine now continued corresponding with Emile, and meeting him in secret at her window. At this time of year it was very cold, and Madeleine would make cups of hot chocolate which she would pass to Emile through the bars. It was in these cups of hot chocolate that she was later accused of having poisoned him. At some time in early February, Madeleine ordered the Smiths' servant boy to visit the pharmacy and obtain a small vial of prussic acid, claiming she needed it for her hands. The servant went to Dr Yeaman's surgery on Sauchiehall Street, but was refused as a physician's authority was required to purchase it. On being told this, Madeleine apparently responded, 'Oh well, never mind.' Madeleine is recorded as having visited Murdoch's on Sauchiehall Street, on 21 February, and purchased arsenic. In the 19th century, the law required that anyone purchasing poison must sign a poison book. Madeleine clearly signed 'M. H. Smith', claiming the arsenic was required to kill rats in the garden and country house. Madeleine put the sixpence worth of arsenic on her father's account and arranged for it to be delivered to the family home later that day.

In early March, Emile was becoming more insistent in his demands for some answers. Madeleine had postponed their marriage without giving what Emile considered a good reason. His letter of 5 March 1857 demanded explicit answers to his questions. The next day, Madeleine was due to meet a school friend, Mary Jane. The girls had been good friends at school in London, and had agreed that when one became engaged, the other would be her bridesmaid. On becoming engaged, Madeleine had written to Mary Jane to announce her engagement and Mary had come to visit. The two girls visited various shops at Sauchiehall Street, before Madeleine asked Mary Jane to stop with her while she went into Currie's the druggists, where she went to purchase sixpence worth of arsenic. Upon being told she would have to sign for it, Madeleine responded, 'Don't worry, I will sign anything you like', before leaving the shop with her purchase. As they left the shop, Mary Jane giggled at the idea of two young women buying arsenic. Madeline laughed along with her.

Mary Perry reported meeting with Emile on 17 February 1857, and stated that he had mentioned he would be meeting Madeleine on 19 February. There are no witness accounts to state this happened, but Emile reported suffering acute stomach pains that night; however, he recovered by the following morning. Emile appeared at his lodgings on the night of 22 February, once again suffering severe stomach pains and sickness; it is not clear where he went on that evening, but subsequently the police chose to link this to Madeleine, based on the time-scales of her arsenic purchases. This time he did not recover so quickly and remained in bed for seven days.

On 6 March, Madeleine is recorded as having purchased more arsenic. On 9 March, Emile reportedly mentioned to his friend, Miss Perry, that he was surprised at feeling so unwell after having 'coffee and chocolate with her'. Miss Perry took this to mean Madeleine, and Emile added, 'Even if she were to poison me, I would still love her.' Miss Perry laughed at Emile and told him not to be foolish. To that, Emile reportedly responded, 'Perhaps she might not be so sorry to get rid of me.'

On 18 March, Madeleine made a further purchase of arsenic. On 19 March, Emile left for a week-long holiday. On 22 March, he appeared back at his lodgings unexpectedly, reporting he had received a letter calling him back, and asked his landlady for a door key, anticipating he would be out late, though he did not specify where he was going. A day later, he was dead. The post-mortem revealed 88 grains of arsenic in his body.

The following morning, the letter summoning him from his holiday was discovered in his coat pocket. It was from Madeleine. This prompted a further search of his lodgings, where a number of letters from Madeleine were discovered. She soon became the subject of local gossip, but maintained a dignified silence; on 26 March, she disappeared.

The family rapidly became frantic. William Minnoch arrived at the family home to pay a visit on his bride-to-be and was informed that she had disappeared. Minnoch suggested that perhaps she had gone to the holiday home where they had first met, and offered to seek her out. William and Jack Smith, Madeleine's brother, went in search of her. As anticipated, Madeleine was indeed hiding in the summer house. William gently questioned her as to why she had run away, and was told by Madeleine that she was feared her parents would be upset by what she had done, and that she would tell him more at a later date. They returned together, though little conversation happened during the journey.

In her absence, the police had uncovered a wealth of evidence against her – primarily the letters she had sent to Emile – and on 31 March, she was arrested.

Under interrogation, Madeleine was surprisingly open. She did not deny her relationship, sexual history, or engagement to Emile l'Angelier, neither did she deny purchasing the arsenic. Her statement specified that she had mixed the arsenic with water and used it to wash her hands and face – a treatment for her complexion that she had learned at her school in London. Her justification for the secrecy was that she was embarrassed, and she declared under oath that she did not administer or cause to be administered, anything that would cause harm to Mr l'Angelier.

The police determined that Madeleine should stand trial for murder, and the case gathered momentum and publicity. It was moved from Glasgow to Edinburgh High Court and began on 30 June 1857. Madeleine was represented by one of the best-known lawyers of the time, John Ingles. In the 19th century women were not allowed to represent themselves in court, and she was therefore solely dependent on Ingles and how he chose to defend her. This may, combined with the fact that it was highly unusual for such a young society woman to be standing trial for murder, have contributed to the media frenzy surrounding her case. People swarmed around outside the court to catch a glimpse of Madeleine as she left to be driven back to jail, and the court was full to capacity every day – there were even tickets available to purchase seats in the halls. The details of Madeleine Smith's trial were the talk of Scotland.

Madeleine was lucky in that some evidence was not allowed into the trial; a lot of this was thanks to John Ingles and his sharp legal brain. Ingles argued that her letters should be allowed, but l'Angelier's diary should not. The prosecution argued strongly for the diary to be allowed, but Ingles argued that it contained dates and entries that implied Madeleine had seen the deceased on specific days. Given that the deceased was dead, the diary could not be challenged and he could not be cross-examined on any point. Therefore, the diary was discounted from the evidence; without it, the prosecution's lack of witnesses to alleged meetings between Madeleine and Emile during the three weeks leading up to his death would prove to be a significant factor in the outcome of the trial.

The trial continued for nine days, with many witnesses, including Madeleine's sister and her (now ex-) fiancé giving evidence. Madeleine's sister (who shared a bedroom with her) insisted that she had not got out of bed on the night of 22 March, and therefore Madeleine could not have seen Emile without waking her sister. In fact, Madeleine's younger sister was an extremely heavy sleeper, which was one of the reasons their dalliances had been able to continue for so long.

A number of witnesses helped the prosecution to highlight the gaps and discrepancies in Madeleine's story; the defence, in turn, summoned witnesses who claimed that Emile had regularly discussed previous suicide attempts. A friend of Emile reported that he had often claimed to be unhappy, and that he had previously stated on a number of occasions that he would 'blow my brains out, if I had the courage'. Another of his acquaintances stated that he talked frequently about the women he entertained, once saying that if he was disappointed, he would not hesitate to drive a knife into his stomach.

A number of experts, including two doctors, discussed the use of arsenic for cosmetic purposes, which helped to discount the prosecution's evidence. One of the more far-fetched theories presented by the defence was that Madeleine may have washed her hands and face with the arsenic, and that Emile may have inadvertently licked it from her. A nonsensical theory, but it all helped to present doubt in the minds of the jurors. The defence and prosecution argued relentlessly.

Madeleine was recognised for her poise and confidence in the courtroom. She refused food or drink, merely requesting some smelling salts, which she did not use. The only sign of weakness was some embarrassment when her letters to Emile, relating directly to their sexual activities, were read aloud. This was understandable, and the content and open sexual discussion in her letters shocked polite Victorian society.

At the end of the trial, the jury took just thirty minutes over their deliberations, returning a verdict of 'Not Proven'. The verdict was a hugely popular one; her defence counsel did not congratulate her, sitting with his head in his hands.

Madeleine was freed that afternoon, and returned to the family home, but the notoriety surrounding the case meant that she was never free of the gossip and soon after fled Scotland, changing her name in the process. Now known as Lena, she went to London with her brother, before moving on to Plymouth. There, she formed a close friendship with a young drawing teacher, George Wardle, who knew her only as Lena. A concerned friend of Wardle's confided the truth to him about Lena's background, but Wardle, something of a romantic, did not care. And so, on 4 July 1861, Madeleine Smith became Lena Wardle. Her father attended the wedding, where it was remarked by a number of guests that he seemed to be deeply melancholy. It appears that James Smith never recovered from the scandal that his daughter had brought upon his family, although he never disowned her.

The Wardles went on to have two children and seemed happy, but in 1889, George Wardle went to live in Italy – without his wife. The reason for this is not known, although some reports say that the marriage was not going smoothly, and that he had seen a look that he did not like in his wife's eye. The marriage ended amicably enough, though the two never met again, and George Wardle died in 1910.

Little is known about Madeleine's life after the breakdown of her marriage. We do know that she decided, at the age of eighty, to emigrate to the United States, where her son Tom was living. Madeleine, or Lena, retained her youthful looks, and could easily pass for twenty years less than her true age, a fact she was particularly proud of. Soon after her arrival, she was proposed to by an elderly Roman Catholic gentleman named Sheehy. Madeleine Smith had now become Lena Wardle Sheehy, and the world seemed to have forgotten Madeleine Smith entirely. That was, until shortly after her husband's death in 1926. Somehow a Hollywood film company had discovered her true identity and wanted to make a film about her life, which she would appear in. When she refused, they threatened to publicly announce her identity and have her removed from the United States as an illegal alien. Even at 90 years old, nobody was going to tell Madeleine Smith what to do, and she remained resolute. Eventually, the film company gave up, preferring to wait for her death before they told her story.

Madeleine Smith died two years later, in 1928, while living in the Bronx, New York. Her tombstone read simply, 'Lena Sheehy'. The full story of Emile l'Angelier's death was a secret that she took to her grave.

THE CASE OF
JESSIE MCLACHLAN

Date: 1862
Place: Glasgow

It was in the early hours of Saturday 5 July 1862 that three sisters, Margaret, Jessie and Peterina McLean, were returning home from their brother's wedding. Their route back into Glasgow took them down Sauchiehall Road, a pleasant tree-lined road of attractive well-kept houses. As they walked, they could see a row of houses in Sandyford Place, separated from the main road only by a row of trees and shrubbery, and they all noticed a light shining through the blinds of the basement of No. 17.

They were not the only people to have noticed the house that night. Mary McIntyre, a local dressmaker, had been walking down Sauchiehall Road just after eleven o'clock the previous evening, when she noticed several people in discussion outside No. 17. They had heard some unsettling noises apparently coming from the house, but not being certain of their origins, they had walked off, leaving Mary alone. As she passed the house she too heard something unsettling – the low moans of someone in pain. She wavered, uncertain whether to enquire into the source of the sounds, but she was alone and it was late, so she walked on.

The house that was the focus of so much attention was that of John Fleming, a successful Glasgow accountant. Fleming was a widower, who lived, in some comfort, at No. 17 with his son, John, his sister, who ran the house for him, and his elderly father, James Fleming, known to all as Old Fleming. Like many successful Glaswegian businessmen, John Fleming had a house in the country, just outside Dunoon on the Firth of Clyde, and this weekend he and his son, a trainee accountant in the family firm, had departed the office in St Vincent Street, and caught the afternoon steamer to Dunoon. As a result, the sole occupants of No. 17 that weekend were Old Fleming, and Jess McPherson, a thirty-five-year-old servant who had been with the family for some years.

The affluent respectability of the Fleming household had only one jarring note – the presence of Old Fleming. His son felt an obligation to house his father, who had, after all, enabled John to receive the education that had elevated him to his current prominent position in society. Old Fleming was given a salary of £40 per year by his son, for which he collected the rents on some of his son's less grand properties, but the truth was that his son found him a social embarrassment. Old Fleming (who claimed to be eighty-seven, but was probably seventy-eight) had started his working life as a hand-loom weaver in Cumbernauld, and although he had subsequently started his own factory, which enabled him to support his family in a reasonable style, he remained stubbornly working class. He spoke broad Scots, and his lack of social graces made him more comfortable eating his meals with the servants. Coupled with this was his partiality to strong spirits, which could lead him, despite his advanced years, to show an unhealthy interest in the female servants. Indeed, only ten years previously, he had been severely censured by the Kirk Session of the Anderson United Presbyterian Church, of which he was the oldest member, for 'the sin of fornication with Janet Dunsmore', a domestic servant who bore his child.

Having enjoyed a relaxing weekend in Dunoon, John Fleming and his son had returned to the city by the early steamer, and had gone straight to the office, so it was not until half past four on the Monday afternoon that John Fleming, the younger, returned to the family home, while his father did some shopping. John was surprised when the front door was opened not by Jess, the servant, but Old Fleming himself. On being asked the whereabouts of the servant, the old man replied, 'She's away. She's cut. I haven't seen her since Friday, and her door's locked.' On being asked whether he had not thought to open the door to check, Old Fleming replied that he had thought she was away visiting friends.

At this stage John Fleming senior arrived home, and on being apprised of the situation by his son, set off for Jess's room in the basement, closely followed by his son and father. He found the door locked and the key missing, but found another key in the pantry which fitted, and so they entered Jess's room. The room was dark, as the blinds were down and the shutters half open, and there, next to the bed, lay the body of Jess McPherson, naked from the waist down, her head and the upper part of her body covered by a piece of carpet. Even a cursory glance could hardly fail to notice the considerable amount of blood spread around the room.

John Fleming rushed upstairs and out on to Sauchiehall Road to raise the alarm; he quickly ran for a doctor living nearby, and it was his butcher who eventually alerted the police. By five o'clock, the police surgeon, Dr Joseph Fleming, was on the scene, and he and the local man, Dr Watson, carried out a careful examination of the body and the basement rooms. In the kitchen, which adjoined the bedroom, a fire was burning. Blood stains were evident in the sink, on the door and high up on the door frame, and a doormat was soaked in blood. Marks in the lobby from the kitchen to the bedroom suggested a body had been dragged along, and there were blood stains in the bedroom, and in other parts of the basement too. It was apparent that an attempt had been made to wash the floors of the kitchen, bedroom and lobby, and also the face, neck, and chest of the deceased. They noted that, although it was apparent that the murder had taken place some days before, the flagstones in the lobby were quite moist, as if the washing had been done recently, and the kitchen floor, although drier, was still perceptibly damp, as were the clothes that remained on the deceased.

The post-mortem the next day confirmed that Jess Mc-Pherson had been murdered with extreme ferocity, although not without a struggle, and that the murderous blows were struck with a cleaver, or similar instrument. Although the number of blows struck was considerable, the post-mortem concluded 'that the comparatively light degree of strength shown in the blows would point to a female or a weak man having inflicted them'.

The continued police investigation of the basement had unearthed some other significant facts. In a room in the basement, where Old Fleming stored his clothes, some of his clean shirts in a chest of drawers showed spots of blood, and the box containing the servant's clothes looked 'as if some bloody hand had been working among them'; in the kitchen drawer was a butcher's cleaver, at first sight clean, but on closer examination showing signs of blood. Finally, on the bedroom floor, beyond the area that had been washed, were three clear imprints of a naked foot, and there was little doubt that they had been made by a female.

* * *

The Flemings had noticed that certain items around the house had gone missing. The final list the police compiled with their help comprised some silver plate and spoons, although it was noted that far more valuable items had been left untouched. In addition, two silk dresses, a jacket and other garments belonging to the deceased were missing. Details of the missing items appeared in the Glasgow newspapers, and were distributed on official handbills.

Despite the suggestion of burglary, and the presence of the bloody female footprints – confirmed as not belonging to the deceased – the police were sufficiently unconvinced of Old Fleming's account of how he could spend three days in a house where a bloody murder had taken place, that the Sheriff of Lanarkshire issued a warrant for his arrest on the charge of being involved in the crime. After four hours of questioning by the Sheriff, he was committed to prison.

During questioning, he confirmed that he had been woken by screams in the early hours of Saturday – four o'clock by his watch – which he put down to unsavoury goings-on on the open ground behind the house. He confirmed also that he had noticed blood spots on his shirts the following morning. Yet despite this, he failed to investigate the matter of the locked door, or to mention Jess's unexpected absence during two visits to church over the weekend, or in conversation with others he had met.

While Old Fleming languished behind bars, the efforts of the police in circulating details of the stolen items had born fruit. Robert Lundie, a Glasgow pawnbroker, had recognised the description of the stolen plate, and told the police that this had been pawned for £6 15s, around midday on the Saturday of the murder, by a woman calling herself Mary McDonald. The name and address given proved false, but on information received – almost certainly from Old Fleming – the police arrested a married couple, James and Jessie McLachlan. The husband, a sailor who was confirmed to have been at sea when the murder took place, was released the following day. Jessie, who had worked for the Flemings for two years, and was a close friend of the deceased, was detained for questioning.

Initially, she denied any knowledge of the crime, or the pawning of the silver plate, but during a four-and-a-half-hour interrogation, stated that she had not been to Sandyford Place at all recently, but that on the Thursday before the murder,

Old Fleming had called at her house, and asked her to pawn some plate and other articles for him, as he needed some cash for a trip to the Highlands, and had told her the name and address to give to the pawnbroker. After she had pawned the items, Old Fleming had returned to her house on the Saturday afternoon to collect the pawn ticket and the money, but then gave her £4 of it, which she used to pay her rent. She gave a detailed account of her movements on the days in question, of the clothes she was wearing, and details of various garments of her own that she had taken in for cleaning and dying. The police, however, had already accumulated a considerable amount of detail about her movements, and were aware that she was lying throughout. As a result, they were able to easily trap her; after Jessie had confirmed that the clothes in question were hers, the police showed her evidence that they were fully aware they were the property of the deceased, at which stage she changed her story to say that Jess had given her the clothes for cleaning. It was not long before more clothes were recovered, some blood-stained, which had been hastily buried.

With evidence starting to pile up against her, the final damning item was the fact that her footprint matched perfectly those found in blood in the bedroom.

As quickly as her trial was scheduled, Old Fleming was released. The newspapers were having a field day – long before the days of a case being considered *sub judice*, they had complete freedom to comment and to express their opinions of the case. While the *Glasgow Herald* rejoiced at the freeing of 'old innocent', the majority of the papers viewed his hasty release with considerable suspicion, suspecting, probably quite rightly, that the Flemings exercised some influence within the higher circles of the forces of law and order. His far from convincing account of his part in the matter had been carefully overlooked, leading to a belief that the main thrust of the investigation had been not so much to find Jessie McLachlan guilty of the murder, as to find Old Fleming innocent.

Jessie's chance of her trial having a successful outcome took a further downturn when it was announced that the trial was set down for the Glasgow autumn circuit. Previous high profile trials involving Glasgow murders had taken place in Edinburgh, to avoid the possibility, or in this case certainty, of local bias. With no form of restraint on the reporting of the trial, the newspapers used it to boost their circulation, in some cases by up to 500%. Evidence was leaked, witnesses interviewed, and endless speculation indulged in, so that the chances of coming up with an impartial jury were slim to none. The final nail in the coffin that seemed sure to await her was the appointment of Lord Deas as the judge presiding. Lord Deas was a judge of great experience and knowledge, but his nickname on the circuit of 'Lord Death' gave a fair indication of his preferred conclusion for a trial.

Some weeks before the trial, Jessie had several meetings with her legal representatives, in which she changed her story once more. Her revised version of events involved her admitting that she had been in No. 17 Sandyford Place on the night of the 4/5 July. Her defence team, having limited knowledge of what evidence the prosecution team had assembled, decided this should not be admitted in court, as placing her firmly at the scene of the crime could weaken her defence.

On 17 September 1862, the trial of Jessie McLachlan commenced at the Old Court in Jail Square, Glasgow. The courthouse was packed, and the participating parties had to fight their way through the crowds outside. Jessie pleaded 'Not Guilty' to the charges brought against her, and her counsel lodged a special defence, 'that the murder alleged in the indictment was committed by James Fleming'.

John Fleming and his son were the first witnesses, outlining the circumstances surrounding their finding of the body,

and then a buzz of excitement passed around the court room
as James Fleming was called to the witness box. The *Morning
Journal* recorded that Old Fleming 'entered the dock nimbly';
actually, he was entering the witness box, the dock being
reserved for the accused, although no doubt some spectators
believed that was where he belonged. The prosecution had
prepared him well; smartly dressed in his black Sunday best,
with luxuriant silver side whiskers, and a pair of glasses supplied for the occasion (he had no need of them), his only
concession to age was slight deafness, which caused him
to give his evidence at some volume. He spoke in a strong
dialect – Doric – the shorthand writer recording a slightly
toned down version for the official records.

According to his testimony, he last saw Jess McPherson alive
on the evening of Friday 4 July. As it was washing day, she was
still hard at work in the kitchen when he retired to his bed at
9.30 p.m. He recounted, as before, the screams that he had
heard and ignored at 4 a.m.; he had gone back to sleep, and
had awoken again at 6 a.m., when it was customary for Jess
to bring him his porridge. Despite her failing to do so, he
remained in bed until 9 a.m., when he arose and dressed. It
was then that he had found her door locked, and received no
response to his knocking. Finding the pantry window open, he
closed it, and made up the fire in the kitchen. The first visitor
of the day, at eleven o' clock, was a maid from the house next
door, seeking to borrow a shovel, and it was at this stage that
he noticed that the front door was shut, but not locked. After
receiving a loaf when the baker called, the old man had left
home at midday to go to the office, and then to one of the
rented properties that he was responsible for, before returning
home by bus. About seven o'clock that evening, a young man
called Darnley called to see Jess, saying he had arranged to do
so when he was next in town, but Fleming told him she was not
in, and he went away. It was at this stage that Fleming went

down to the basement and removed his shirts from where they had been drying, and noticed the blood on them. After a light supper, he retired to bed at nine o'clock.

On the Sunday morning, he heard the front doorbell ring, which he knew would be the milkman, but he didn't get up to answer it. After breakfast he attended church, and then again in the afternoon for divine service. That evening, Jess's young man Darnley called and was turned away again, and so Fleming retired to bed, at 9.30 p.m. once more. Monday was a busy day for him collecting rents, before returning home at about two o'clock, and finding the body with his son and grandson little more than two hours later.

He was able to identify the pawned plate, but denied giving it to Jessie McLachlan to pawn, as he was in no need of money, having £150 in the Glasgow Savings Bank, and £30 in the Royal Bank of Scotland. He stated that although he knew Jessie McLachlan from when she was employed by his son three years before, the only occasion when he had seen her since was when he once visited her house. (It was pointed out in the press, subsequently, that when he had first been confronted with her on his examination by the Sheriff, he denied even knowing her.)

Andrew Rutherfurd-Clark, cross-examining for the defence, sought confirmation of the events of the Saturday morning – that Old Fleming's watch was right, that he rose at nine, and that the first visitor was next door's maid at eleven o'clock, at which stage he noticed the front door to be unlocked. The old man confirmed this all to be true. It was then that Rutherfurd-Clark asked the question that proved to have considerable significance in due course – did the milkman call on Saturday morning, as well as Sunday morning? This proved a difficult question to get an answer to. Having denied, on seven previous occasions, that the milkman called, Old Fleming was finally forced to admit that the milk-boy had rung the doorbell between eight and nine o'clock, and that he had opened the door, on the chain, while fully dressed, and declined the offer of milk, although subsequently revising this to say he could not recall whether he was dressed or not. Lord Deas, having taken an active part in questioning witnesses up to this point, had refrained from asking Old Fleming for any clarification of his testimony, and had sought to protect him as far as possible from the hostile cross-examination he was under-going from the defence counsel. On being asked repeatedly by Mr Rutherfurd-Clark on why he had promptly answered the door to the milkman, when he might reasonably have expected Jess to do this as usual, he gave answers that seemed to imply that she was already dead, before hastily denying he was aware of this, and finally blaming his old age for a failing memory. The prosecution were no doubt relieved when Lord Deas released Old Fleming from the witness box at the earliest possible opportunity.

*   *   *

The case against Jessie McLachlan went altogether more smoothly for the prosecution. A steady stream of witnesses was called, and they ripped her statements to shreds. Despite stating she did not leave her house on the Friday, witnesses stated that they had seen her out, and indeed she told one she was on her way to see Jess McPherson, and walked with her part of the way. She had left home at ten o'clock, and had told the witness she left it late to visit, to make sure Old Fleming was safely in bed before she arrived. She was seen to return home around 9 o'clock on the Saturday morning carrying a bundle, and was seen to leave shortly after wearing different clothes. The court heard how she had pawned the items for £6 15s, had used £4 for her arrears of rent, and the process by which she had attempted to dispose of the deceased's clothes, and her own bloodstained clothes. During cross-examination, the defence attempted to raise the matter of the scandal involving Old Fleming ten years before, but the judge quickly quashed the line of questioning.

Finally, the prosecution case was complete, and it was the turn of the defence. By comparison, the witnesses called were small in number. George Paton, the milkman, confirmed he had called between half past seven and twenty to eight on the Saturday morning, and also on the Sunday and Monday, but, unusually, no milk was required on any of the days. Donald McQuarrie, the milk-boy, confirmed the he had rung the bell once, and the door was opened on the chain promptly by old Mr Fleming, who was dressed in black clothes. He had not known Old Fleming to have answered the door before.

Mary Smith, a close friend of the deceased for some six years, had met her a few days before her death, and commented that she looked unwell. Jess replied that, 'I do not feel very happy or comfortable with Old Mr Fleming, for he is actually an old wretch and an old devil.' When Mrs Smith mentioned she looked ill, Jess declined to tell her the reason in front of Mrs Smith's husband. Mrs McKinnon, the sister of the deceased, recounted more adverse comment from her sister regarding Old Fleming. Martha McIntyre, another servant at the Fleming house, confirmed her disquiet about Old Fleming, and his particular obsession with the affairs of the deceased.

In summing up for the prosecution, Mr Gifford for the Crown reiterated the lies identified in the testimony of the accused, and reminded the jury that it was she, and not Old Fleming, who was on trial. The summary for the defence was more difficult. Mr Rutherfurd-Clark had hoped the prosecution would not be able to prove his client had been to the murder house (despite him knowing full well that she had), but the bloody footprints had been a bad setback. On completion of his summing up, at nine o'clock on the evening of the third day of the trial, the court adjourned, ready for the conclusion the following day.

When Lord Deas took his seat in court the next morning, it was hard to miss the black cap he was carrying, and which he placed prominently on the bench before him. He started to address the jury at ten-thirty, and concluded at two twenty-five. Those watching in court were of the opinion that he expressed the case for the prosecution better than the prosecution. The jury, left in little doubt of his lordship's requirements, took no more than fifteen minutes to announce a unanimous vote of 'Guilty'.

* * *

It was at this stage in the proceedings that events took an unusual turn. On hearing the verdict, Jessie McLachlan beckoned to her counsel, and the court was asked if she may be allowed to make a statement. Rising to her feet, and addressing the court for the first time, she spoke clearly: 'I desire to have it read, my Lord. I am as innocent as my child, who is only three years of age at this date.' Mr Rutherfurd-Clark rose to make the statement, which was the one she had dictated to her defence counsel weeks before the trial, and which had remained suppressed.

Her story gave a very different account of the events of the night of 4/5 July. She had made her way to Sandyford Place, as the prosecution had alleged, to find, to her disappointment, that Old Fleming was still up, and sitting with Jess in the kitchen. Producing a bottle of whisky, they shared drinks until the bottle was gone, so Old Fleming gave Jessie the money to have the bottle refilled, but the lateness of the hour meant she found the local public house shut, and so she returned empty-handed. On finding the back door shut, she knocked and was let in by Old Fleming. There was no sign of the servant, and Jessie intended to go home, when she heard moaning coming from the bedroom, and there she found Jess McPherson on the floor semi-conscious, with a large wound across her forehead, and cuts on her nose. Old Fleming said that he had not intended to hurt her, and that it had been an accident, and went to fetch water. As Jessie bathed her face, he left the room and came back with a basin of water, and started to scrub the blood from the floor, spilling the basin and soaking Jessie McLachlan's boots in the process. Jess began to recover a little, and declined the offer of a doctor. Together they helped Jess onto the bed, and Jessie took off her boots to let them dry in the kitchen. Later, Jess recovered sufficiently to tell the story of what happened. Some weeks ago, Old Fleming had returned drunk one night, climbed into her bed, and attempted to take advantage of her. She had rebuffed his attentions, but there had been tension between them ever since, as he feared she would tell his son of his misconduct. When Jessie had left in search of whisky, the row had flared again, and he had struck her in the face.

When Jessie went off to confront the old man, he begged her not to tell anyone of what had occurred, promising he would make her 'comfortable all of her life', and making her swear on the bible that she would keep her silence. Jess was by that time complaining of cold, so together they managed to get her to the kitchen where they laid her on a couch in front of the fire. By four o'clock on Saturday morning, her condition had begun to deteriorate and she asked for a doctor, but Old Fleming refused to let Jessie leave. It was while she was trying to see if she could attract the attention of any passers-by from the parlour window that she heard noises from the kitchen, and returned to see Jess lying on the floor, and Old Fleming striking at her with a meat cleaver. Fearing for her own safety, she screamed and ran upstairs, followed by the old man, telling her not to be afraid. He had formulated a plan. If she maintained her silence, he would say that he had found the house robbed when he awoke in the morning, and would leave the larder window open to support his story. If she refused, then he would accuse her of the crime. He had dragged the body back into the bedroom, washed himself, and burned his blood-stained clothes on the fire. After the milkman had called, at 8.30 a.m. he hustled her out of the back gate with the items to pawn and Jess's clothes, to simulate the burglary, promising as she left to set her up in a shop, and to never see her want.

The reading of the document had taken forty minutes in the hushed court, but if anyone had any thought that it might have some impact on the outcome of the trial, Lord Deas did not share them. Outlining his theory on how she had butchered her friend, he was completely in agreement with the verdict. 'There is not in my mind a shadow of suspicion that the old gentleman had anything whatever to do with the murder.' Donning the black cap, he pronounced that Jessie McLachlan be returned to prison, and kept on a diet of bread and water, until 11 October, when she would be hanged – 'And may God Almighty have mercy on your soul.' 'Mercy!' was Jessie's response, 'Aye, He'll ha'e mercy, for I'm innocent.'

The trial provoked a storm of controversy. While a few newspapers praised the way Lord Deas had conducted proceedings, the vast majority felt that justice had not been done. Soon a petition raised in Glasgow had 50,000 signatures, and Old Fleming was banished to the family's country house in Dunoon to prevent further altercations breaking out, although even there he was recognised and chased through the streets by a mob.

On the instructions of the Lord Advocate, a private investigation into the case was started, and a week before the scheduled date for the hanging, a letter from the Home Office deferred it to 1 November. The case was the subject of two long debates in the House of Commons, and further inquiry was instigated.

The original trial called upon seventy-six witnesses, the inquiry called upon sixty-nine, some of whom were new, including the three sisters who were passing early Saturday morning on the day of the murder. The enquiry found that Jessie's statement that was read out in court seemed to tally with such facts that were known, and on 6 November the death sentence was commuted to penal servitude for life.

*   *   *

Jessie McLachlan completed the statutory fifteen-year sentence in H.M. General Prison of Perth, and on 5 October 1877 she walked free, at the age of forty-four, with the £30 she had earned in jail. Her husband and her son had emigrated after the trial, so she went to stay with a cousin in Greenock, but could not shake off the attentions of the newspapers. Eventually she fled to the United States, and died in Port Huron, Michigan, on New Year's Day 1899, at the age of sixty-six.

The truth about what really happened that night in Sandyford Place will never be known. Rumours persisted that after the death sentence was commuted, Jessie made another (her fifth) account of the events to her legal counsel, in which she stated she was responsible for the murder under the influence of laudanum, and that Old Fleming was blameless. But like her other stories, this, as it was reported, was riddled with inconsistencies, and could be another example of her inability to state the truth. What does seem reasonably certain is that the central figure in the affair, thanks to family influence, escaped scot-free.

THE RATHO MURDERER

Date: 1864
Place: Edinburgh

Unlike many of the accused in this book, there was no question of the guilt of George Bryce, his bloody deed witnessed by terrified onlookers. There is also no question that if judged by our modern understanding of mental illness, he would never have gone to the gallows. But it is for the manner of his death that his name is remembered.

George Bryce was the son of John and Agnes Bryce (née Fraser),* born and raised in the village of Ratho, near Edinburgh. His father was a successful businessman, who had made his money from various sources, being a coal merchant, haulage contractor, spirit dealer and farmer. He employed his son as a porter. At the time, Bryce was described as 'simple', but apart from that convenient label, there was no knowledge of, or treatment for, his condition. He had attempted suicide on a number of occasions, and his heavy drinking did nothing to help the severe mood swings that he was subject to.

In 1863 George, then in his late twenties, started working at Ratho Villa, a large house that was the property of Robert Tod, a local grain merchant. Bryce was a heavily-built rather plain man, but before long he had started a relationship with Lizzie Brown, who worked as a cook at the house. He courted Lizzie for some time, and hoped to marry her, but she cooled towards him, and the other servants disapproved of the affair. One in particular, Jeanie Seaton, warned her that Bryce was not to be trusted. In March of 1864, George, Lizzie, Jeanie and some others had gone to Edinburgh to see the

illuminations put up in honour of the wedding of the Prince
and Princess of Wales. George had been drinking heavily,
and believed he heard Jeanie refer to him as a 'drunken
blackguard'. Jeanie attempted to smooth things over, but
when Lizzie broke off the relationship shortly after, Jeanie
Seaton was firmly established in Bryce's mind as the reason for
Lizzie's refusal of his proposal of marriage.

On 16 April 1864, George Bryce returned to Ratho Villa.
Robert Tod was away on business, leaving Mrs Tod and the
servants as the only occupants of the house. Bryce searched the
house until he found Jeanie Seton, and started to beat her
mercilessly with his fists. Her screams brought the members of
the household running, and they found him with his hands
around her throat, attempting to stifle her cries. The servants
managed to pull him off her, Mrs Tod thrashing at him with an
umbrella, and Jeanie Seton, released from his grasp, rushed
from the house seeking safety in a nearby cottage. Bryce broke
away from the servants, and set off in pursuit. Before she could
reach the safe haven of the cottage, he caught her, and throwing
her to the ground, drew a razor from his pocket and savagely
cut her throat. Bryce fled, leaving her body slumped on the path
of the cottage. The servants rushed to her aid, but she bled to
death. A group of villagers set off in pursuit, and Bryce was soon
caught and taken to Calton Jail.

The violence of the act caused the trial of 'The Ratho
Murderer' to attract much comment in the newspapers, and
amongst the general public. Bryce pleaded 'Not Guilty by
Reason of Insanity', and his family testified to his mental
problems as demonstrated by his various suicide attempts,
but the outcome was a formality. The jury took only forty-
five minutes to return with a 'Guilty' verdict, although they
made some acknowledgement of his condition by recom-
mending his execution be as merciful as possible in view
of 'the low organisation of his mental faculties'. He was

sentenced to death by hanging, to take place at Lawnmarket in Edinburgh on 21 June.

On 20 June, Bryce was transferred to the prison in Parliament Square, and spent his last night sleeping fitfully, from time to time singing psalms with the prison officers. The following morning, perhaps with relief that his years of mental anguish were soon to be over, he told his warders that he had just spent 'the happiest night of my life'.

As was customary, the hanging would be held in full view of the public. One recent change to the scaffold was that there was a black screen erected on three sides, so that when the condemned man dropped through the trap door, his final moments would not be seen, but otherwise everything proceeded in the usual way. A crowd of between 20,000 and 30,000 people had begun to assemble, with everyone seeking the best vantage point to follow the action. As was traditional, the crowd would bring food to sustain them while they waited for the main event to commence, together with a good supply of rotten fruit and vegetables. The young age of the victim and the barbarity of the crime ensured the crowd were ready to give more than just verbal abuse.

As the small procession escorting the prisoner appeared, the crowd reached fever pitch; to an ear-splitting chorus of jeers, Bryce made his way to the gallows under a shower of stones and vegetable matter, whispering to himself 'perfectly composed, perfectly composed'. In previous years, the execution would have been carried out by a professional hangman retained by the City Council – the 'Final Executioner of the Law' – but after the murder of the last occupant of the post, it was decided to bring in executioners from outside the area. As a result, the man in charge was Thomas Askern, who normally performed his duties in York. Whether his failings as a hangman were due to ineptitude or drunkenness is not clear, but what is clear is that the execution went badly wrong. Over the years, the hangman's

art had been refined so that the careful placement of the knot of
the noose and the carefully calculated drop would break the
victim's neck, and death would be instantaneous.

In the event, when the trapdoor opened, and Bryce plunged
through it and the rope snapped tight, his neck did not break.
The execution took place at 8.20 a.m., but Bryce was not pronounced dead until 9.00 a.m. The mood of the crowd, desperate
to see his life ended at first, gradually quietened as they began
to understand the appalling spectacle they were witnessing,
finally turning to anger. The substantial police presence barely
prevented a full-scale riot taking place. The executioner was
hurriedly removed from the scene, and smuggled from the city
in disguise later in the day.

The newspapers made little of the incident, but no one who
witnessed it would ever forget it. The City Council were
determined that such a spectacle, and the resulting threat of civil
unrest, would never occur again. Their views reflected a changing attitude in society. In 1864, a Royal Commission was set up
to consider capital punishment, and when it concluded in 1866,
included a recommendation that public executions should cease.
The Capital Punishment Amendment Act became law in 1868.

The modern-day visitor to Edinburgh, walking the Royal
Mile, will see the following sign:

SITE OF THE LAST PUBLIC EXECUTION IN EDINBURGH

*The site of the gallows is marked by the three brass
plates set at the edge of the pavement in front of this
notice. George Bryce, the Ratho Murderer, was
executed here on 21 June 1864, the last public
execution in Edinburgh.*

---

* The newspaper reports at the time incorrectly stated his parents to be James
and Catherine Bryce. Our thanks go to Tom Bryce for providing the documen-
tation which enabled us to correct this error from the first edition of this book.

THE HUMAN CROCODILE

Date: 1865
Place: Edinburgh

Dr Edward William Pritchard was born in Hampshire in 1825 into a respectable and well-regarded naval family. His father was a navy captain, and two of his uncles were admirals; one of his brothers was secretary to the naval commander-in-chief in Plymouth, with another brother being a navy surgeon. Not surprisingly, he was expected to follow in the family tradition with a navy-based career. At fifteen years of age, he was apprenticed to surgeons in Portsmouth. Keen to become a doctor, he undertook further medical studies in London, before joining the navy.

Pritchard's medical qualifications are somewhat questionable in their validity. He claimed to have attended King's College in London to complete his hospital studies, but subsequent searches of college records have failed to identify a student with his name in 1843. However, it seems clear that he must have obtained some kind of medical training as, on 29 May 1846, he appeared in front of the College of Examiners, and, after examination, was admitted to the College. Later in 1846, he was examined by the Navy Board, and subsequently offered the position of Assistant Naval Surgeon. Pritchard served on a number of ships, including the H.M.S. *Victory* during her final days.

In 1850 he was aboard H.M.S. *Hecate*, which sailed into Portsmouth. On disembarking for leave, Pritchard and a number of other sailors were invited to a ball in the town. Pritchard was introduced to a pretty young woman named

Mary Jane Taylor. Mary was the daughter of an Edinburgh silk merchant, and was in Portsmouth visiting her uncle, Dr David Cowan. David Cowan was a retired navy surgeon, which is how he and Mary came to be at the ball. Mary and Edward soon fell in love, and after a brief courtship, Pritchard proposed marriage. Delighted, Mary accepted, and Pritchard was taken to meet her parents in Edinburgh.

Edward Pritchard was a handsome man, with considerable personality and presence. Flamboyant and generous, the young doctor quickly charmed Mary's parents, who deemed him a suitable partner for their daughter. Pritchard's mother-in-law in particular took to him immediately, and thought the world of him. Pritchard had not finished his service in the navy, and not having sufficient funds to buy himself out, he was forced to return to H. M. S. *Hecate*. Mary accompanied him when possible, but they were often apart for extended periods, with Mary staying in Edinburgh with her parents. Mary's parents could see how unhappy this made their daughter, and were determined to get him ashore permanently. They paid for his release from the navy, and provided a significant sum of money to help the young couple start their life together. This was not the last time that the Taylors would help Pritchard financially.

Pritchard opened a small country medical practice in Hunmanby in Yorkshire, where the couple settled and started a family. Pritchard was ambitious, and extended his practice to the nearby town of Filey. Keen to boost his reputation, Pritchard joined the Freemasons in nearby Scarborough, where he rose to the position of Master of the Royal Lodge in 1857, and Master of Old Globe Lodge in 1858 and 1859. While in Yorkshire, Pritchard wrote a number of books about his travels, and published a number of articles in the medical journal *The Lancet*.

By the time they moved to Glasgow in 1860, Mary Jane and Edward had three sons and two daughters. There are various accounts of the reasons behind the move. Some say that Pritchard despised life as a small country doctor and wished to return to a larger city. Others suggest rumours of inappropriate conduct with female patients and financial problems. Colleagues of Pritchard later stated that while he appeared to be a respectable family man, he was widely regarded among his colleagues as 'a joke' due to his frequent boasting and lying. Pritchard would tell a number of tall tales to locals, but it was said he was succeeding only in deceiving himself. In small towns like Hunmanby and Filey, dramatic lies such as Pritchard's were quickly dismissed as improbable. He had an immense sense of self-importance, and often arranged for his groom to call for him during church services, where he would disrupt proceedings by leaving dramatically and riding noisily away. He openly declared himself to be an excellent lover; quite what Mary made of all this is not known. The family left Yorkshire under a dark cloud, leaving behind considerable debts. If Pritchard was hoping that a move would leave trouble behind, he was mistaken – it followed the family to Glasgow.

On moving to Scotland, the couple stayed with Mary's parents in Edinburgh for a short time while they waited for their new home in Glasgow to become ready. The Taylors remained blissfully unaware of any problems, and referred to their son-in-law as an idol. By now, Pritchard had become a Doctor of Medicine by purchasing a number of diplomas from the University of Erlangen in Germany. He followed this by becoming a Licentiate of the Society of Apothecaries of London; he felt now that he had sufficient qualifications to set himself up in any practice in the country, having sold his practices in Hunmanby and Filey. He was residing with the Taylors following a bout of illness, having felt under the weather for some time, and on the advice of Michael Taylor, took some time off to travel. He accompanied an acquaintance of Mary's father across Egypt and the Holy Land, while working for him as a medical attendant. He returned refreshed and in excellent health, and decided to take the advice of Mary's parents and set up in practice in Glasgow.

With the family settled in Glasgow, Pritchard set about attempting to ingratiate himself into Glasgow's élite medical circles. Despite his having a number of diplomas, and holding letters of introduction to eminent medical doctors in Glasgow, the medical fraternity regarded him with suspicion. He attempted to join the Faculty of Physicians and Surgeons, but could find nobody to sponsor him. Having failed at this, he attempted to join various medical societies – all that was generally needed to achieve this was an adequate diploma and a decent character, but once again, he failed. Undeterred, he set his sights on becoming part of the élite Glasgow social circles. Finally, he succeeded in joining the exclusive Glasgow Athenaeum club, and was so dedicated a member that he was appointed a director. He also became a member of the Society of Arts, and regularly gave lectures on his travels. He particularly liked to lecture on his visits to Fiji; it was wryly commented by an acquaintance that Fiji seemed to be an entirely different place each time he discussed it.

He tried to win approval by telling stories of his connections, claiming that his brother was the Governor-General of Ceylon. When this proved unsuccessful, he claimed a close personal friendship with General Garibaldi, the great Italian liberator. He carried a cane with the inscription, 'From Gen. Garibaldi to Edward William Pritchard'. The effect of this was somewhat limited, as a number of acquaintances recollected seeing him carrying the same cane some months previously, at which time the inscription was notably missing. He told tall stories of his time in the navy, once claiming: 'I have plucked eaglets from their eyries in the deserts of Arabia and hunted the Nubian lion on the prairies of North America'. For an assistant navy surgeon, such stories seemed very unlikely.

By 1863, Pritchard was living with his family at 11 Berkeley Square. The house was large enough comfortably to accommodate Pritchard, Mary and their five children, and even included some attic space which was shared by two servant girls, Elizabeth McGinn and another maid whose name is unknown. On 6 May 1863, at around 3 a.m., a policeman on patrol noticed a fire in the attic of the house. He pounded loudly on the door to raise the alarm. Pritchard was roused, and reported later that he ran up the stairs calling Elizabeth's name. He was unable to rescue her, as the flames approaching the attic were too intense and he could not pass them. The fire was contained, and no major damage occurred to the rest of the house, but Elizabeth McGinn could not be saved. She was found dead in bed, her face, torso and arms horribly charred. Her legs were encased in stockings, and escaped significant damage from the fire.

The official cause of the fire was a gas jet igniting – in theory from a lamp as she read in bed. The odd condition and position of her body provoked suspicion, as did the fact that the fire was determined to have started in her bedroom, yet she had made no attempt to escape. Could the girl have been drugged, unconscious or even already dead when the fire started? Stockings seemed unusual garments to wear to bed – could she have been murdered and then placed in the bed after her death? In the neighbourhood, tongues wagged; rumours abounded that the girl was pregnant and having an affair with Pritchard. Concerned police officers heard the rumours, and found it especially suspicious that the fire had started when both Mary Pritchard and the other servant girl were out of the house.

An investigation was carried out, and Pritchard was questioned at length. It seems likely that the doctor knew more about the circumstances than he claimed, but no action was taken and the insurance claim made by Pritchard was duly honoured. The good doctor may well have got away with murder. Dogged with rumours and gossip, the family sensibly decided to move house. They moved to a house a short distance away, 22 Royal Crescent.

Pritchard's high opinion of himself continued to grow. It was around this time he developed the bizarre habit of walking the streets of Glasgow, handing postcards containing his own photograph to those that he considered worthy of the honour.

The family settled into their new home, and a servant named Mary McLeod was hired. McLeod was a pretty fifteen-year-old, originating from Islay. Pritchard quickly set his sights on the girl. Despite being nearly 25 years her senior, he became determined to seduce her. By this point, Pritchard had lost the looks that had attracted his wife to him in 1850. Previously an imposing figure standing at six feet tall, he now walked with a stoop. He was rapidly balding, a fact he attempted to disguise by cultivating a somewhat ridiculous comb-over, and growing a massive beard (though no moustache), perhaps to compensate for the lack of hair on his head.

In 1864, Mary and the children took a summer holiday in Dunoon, and Pritchard, seizing his chance, seduced his attractive young servant girl. Amid more rumours of impropriety between Pritchard and his lady patients, the family moved again, this time to the exclusive Sauchiehall Street. By this time, Pritchard's finances were shaky. The house cost £2,000, of which £500 was covered by Mary's mother, and the rest was raised on a loan and an overdraft. On the face of things, the couple appeared to have a loving relationship. However, the affair between Pritchard and the servant, Mary McLeod, continued, and the situation worsened when the fifteen-year-old became pregnant. The enterprising Pritchard told the girl that he loved her, and if his wife were to die before he did, then he would marry her. On the strength of this promise, the girl permitted the doctor to carry out an abortion. Mary McLeod admitted the affair with her employer to a washerwoman with whom she was friendly. She also confirmed that she had been pregnant and lost the baby, and that Pritchard had been kind to her, leading to speculation that Pritchard was the father. It is reported that in October, Pritchard landed himself in hot water when his wife caught the pair kissing.

Very soon after this, in November 1864, Mary Jane Pritchard fell ill with vomiting and diarrhoea. Her husband diagnosed her with gastric fever, though it should be noted that on 16 November, Pritchard had purchased an ounce of tartarised antimony, and a week later, a tincture of aconite. Both these substances were deadly poisons. Coincidentally, Pritchard bought these items from Murdoch's and Currie's in Sauchiehall Street, the same shops that had sold arsenic to Madeleine Smith several years before.

After being ill for some time, Mary Jane decided to return to her parents' home in Edinburgh, where her mother would be able to care for her. Mary began to get better almost immediately, and was soon fully recuperated; she was able to return to Glasgow to spend a happy Christmas with her family. Shortly after, she became ill once again with the same complaint. She suffered the worst symptoms just after her meals, especially when she had eaten a liquid food, such as soup. Her condition was so weakened that she would rarely be well enough to attend meals with her family, instead having Pritchard take her meals to her room.

In February 1865, she suffered a more serious attack of illness, which was witnessed by the family cook, Catherine Lattimer. Lattimer was actually working her last day in the Pritchards' employment, having been fired by Edward Pritchard, when he discovered her giving leftover food to a poor washerwoman. Mary had managed to get down to the dining room for lunch, but as the cook cleared up the dishes, she heard Mary groaning in the pantry. Catherine was much alarmed as she helped her mistress to bed. Mary was doubled over in pain from the cramps, and told her she had never felt so bad before. Catherine ran to fetch Pritchard.

The next day, Dr Pritchard wrote to Mary's cousin, a retired doctor, requesting a second opinion; Dr Cowan duly arrived a few days later. By this point, Mary had improved significantly, and Dr Cowan did not consider her condition at all serious. On examining his cousin, he diagnosed a stomach irritation. He prescribed a mustard poultice, and small amounts of champagne and ice. He also suggested that Mary's mother should come to Glasgow and spend some time with her. Pritchard took heed of the advice and purchased the champagne. However, he also purchased another ounce of antimony and one of aconite. Mary's condition did not improve and over the course of February, she became progressively worse.

Before her mother arrived, Mary had another severe attack during the night. She was overheard by Catherine Lattimer, who was due to have left the Pritchard home some weeks before, but had agreed to stay on pending a replacement being found, as her mistress was so unwell. She entered Mrs Pritchard's room and found her in a hysterical state, demanding to see Dr Gairdner, who was Professor of Med-icine at Glasgow University, and had once been a classmate of her brother at university; Dr Gairdner was duly sent for. On arrival, he was shocked at the state of Mary, and initially determined that she must be drunk. However, he was troubled by her hands, which were outside of the bedclothes with the wrists and fingers so distorted they looked more like claws. Gairdner diagnosed her as drunk and hysterical. He recommended a course of treatment consisting exclusively of bread, milk and hard-boiled eggs. However, he suspected the possibility that Mary might be being poisoned, and wrote to Mary's brother to suggest as much. Even if she was not being poisoned, he very much disapproved of the treatment she was receiving, and recommended she be moved to hospital or to the home of her brother, Dr Taylor. Dr Taylor agreed with the assessment, and wrote to Pritchard to request she be moved to his home. Pritchard responded that while he was delighted with the suggestion, Mary was, unfortunately, too ill to be moved.

This was not surprising, as antimony poisoning was the cause of her condition. Records have revealed Pritchard continued to buy vast quantities of both tartarised antimony and tincture of aconite over the months of her illness. By now, Mary's mother had arrived to look after her and help with the running of the house. It is not clear why Mary was not transferred to hospital, but Pritchard's mother-in-law had always been particularly fond of him, and may not have believed him capable of harming his wife.

Shortly after, Mrs Taylor herself became ill, with the same symptoms as her daughter. It is reported that Mary, her mother and also the cook became ill after eating tapioca pudding. Mary's elderly mother had another health problem – she had formed a dependency on an opium-based solution, Battley's Sedative Solution, which was taken for general aches and pains. While staying with her daughter, she worked her way through a three-month supply in just a fortnight. As her daughter's health continued to go downhill, Mrs Taylor also deteriorated. Playing the part of the concerned son-in-law, Pritchard called for another local doctor to examine her. Dr James Paterson obliged, and determined that she was under the influence of a large quantity of opium and was dying.

As it turned out, Pritchard had taken advantage of her dependency, and had secretly been administering huge doses of opium to both his wife and mother-in-law.

For Pritchard, the timing of Paterson's visit proved fortuitous, as Mrs Taylor died just hours after he left on 24 February

1865. Dr Pritchard himself signed the death certificate, citing the cause of death as 'Primary cause, Paralysis: duration, twelve hours. Secondary cause, Apoplexy: duration, one hour.' After her death, a number of servants went to Mrs Taylor's room to 'dress' the body. One of the servants discovered a bottle of Battley's Sedative Solution in a drawer. Pritchard entered the room and asked the servant for the bottle. Upon finding it half empty, he expressed dismay at the quantity she had consumed in just a week, and asked the servant not to discuss the bottle with anyone, as it would not do for him and his family to be gossiped about. The body was then transported to Edinburgh for the funeral. Pritchard attended, perhaps in part to reassure himself that she was safely buried. Mary was too ill to attend.

On his return to Glasgow after the funeral, Pritchard noticed no improvement in his wife's health; in fact her condition appeared to be worsening. On 13 March he wrote to his eldest daughter, who was living in Edinburgh at the time, to notify her that her mother was still unwell. By now, it appears that Mrs Pritchard may have had firm suspicions that she was being poisoned, and her strange symptoms began to affect others in the household. Some days before her death, Mary McLeod took her some cheese for her supper. Mary Pritchard asked her to taste a small piece of the cheese, which Mary McLeod duly did. She reported a strange burning sensation in her throat. The next morning, the new cook, Mary Patterson, also ate some of the cheese and became so sick she was forced to retire to bed.

The next night, Mr Pritchard asked the cook to make some egg flip for Mrs Pritchard – egg flip being a Scottish drink, similar to egg nog – saying that he would get some sugar for the drink. He was seen going to the dining room where the sugar was kept, before ducking into his consulting room. He then returned with two sugar lumps, which he dropped into the egg flip. Upon tasting it, the cook commented on the horrid bitter taste of the drink.

On 17 March, Mary Pritchard suffered from a severe attack of cramps and became extremely light-headed. A witness later reported that, just prior to this attack, her husband had given her a tonic. A servant later tasted the concoction, and became violently ill. Mary's condition then took a sharp downturn, and in an apparent panic, Pritchard once again called Dr James Paterson to examine her. Paterson did so, and prescribed a solution to help her sleep. Pritchard asked him to dictate the contents of the solutions, proclaiming that he kept no medicines in the house except for Battley's Solution and chloroform, so the ingredients would need to be fetched from the chemist. Having done all he could, Paterson left. The list never made it to the chemist, and Pritchard returned to his wife. That night, he slept in the bed with his ailing wife, expressing a great show of love and concern. Mary died just a few hours later.

Pritchard appeared distressed, first ordering the cook, Mary Patterson, to bring a mustard poultice. Mary awkwardly pointed out that it would do no good to apply a poultice to a dead body. Pritchard then asked for hot water. Mary once again stated that hot water would not help when the person was dead. Pritchard then appeared confused, asking, 'Are you saying she is dead?' Mary responded, 'Doctor, you should know this better than I.'

At this point, Pritchard broke down in tears, lamenting the death of his beloved wife and asked that a rifle be brought, and for someone to shoot him. Patterson refused, and Pritchard responded that she was a good and kind woman. Next, Pritchard went downstairs and wrote two letters. Exhibiting slightly strange behaviour for a man who had just moments ago appeared so distraught, he wrote one letter to his bank, who had written to him some days ago regarding his overdraft, to confirm that he had suffered the death of his wife that very day, and that he would arrange an appointment shortly after her funeral had taken place.

Pritchard asked Dr Paterson to sign the death certificate, but Paterson refused, stating that he was not present at the time of death, and could not clearly detail a cause of death. Undeterred, Pritchard signed the certificate himself. Appearing to be devastated at the death of his wife, Pritchard arranged for his wife's body to be transferred to Edinburgh, to be buried in the family tomb alongside her mother.

Pritchard travelled to Edinburgh to make the final arrangements for his wife's funeral. He played the part of the bereaved husband exceptionally well. As Mary lay in her coffin in her father's house in Edinburgh, Pritchard requested that the coffin be opened one more time, and kissed his dead wife's lips tenderly as a final farewell. Onlookers reported that he appeared desolate, and wept openly as he paid his last respects.

After the funeral, he headed back to Glasgow by train, where he was stunned to be greeted on the platform at Queen Street Station by Detective Superintendent McCall of the Glasgow City Police. Pritchard was read his rights before being arrested for the murders of his wife and mother-in-law. His arrest followed an anonymous tip-off sent to the procurer fiscal, which raised suspicions that the women had not died of natural causes, but been poisoned. It is almost certain that the tip-off came from Dr James Paterson, who had been asked to sign both death certificates. His refusal to put his name to anything surrounding the deaths of the women seems telling.

Despite some of his odd personality traits, Pritchard had become a generally well-respected doctor, and his trial for double murder caused a sensation. The trial took place in the Edinburgh High Court, presided over by Lord Inglis. It lasted for four days, and was full of extensive examination and cross-examination. By this point, it was largely accepted that both Mary Jane Pritchard and her mother had died of poisoning. Prior to the trial, Mrs Taylor's body had been exhumed and both bodies were duly examined. Huge quantities of antimony were discovered in both, which was not an ingredient contained in Battley's Sedative Solution. The distribution of the poison throughout Mrs Pritchard's body provided damning evidence that she had been slowly poisoned over an extended period. Unable to deny the fact of the poisonings, Pritchard's defence team sought to blame them on the servant, Mary McLeod, who had briefly been taken into custody in the early part of the investigation, but had been released after two days. Pritchard consistently proclaimed his innocence, and was staunchly supported by his relatives and friends, as well as the general public in the early part of the trial. One paper reported later: 'No one who saw the intelligent, thoughtful and mild-looking individual seated in the dock on the first morning, could be prepared for anything like the consummate villainy and diabolic cruelty which each day brought to light . . . the whole murderous plot.'

Several pharmacists were called as witnesses in the trial, and it was confirmed that a doctor could acquire large quantities of antimony without arousing a great deal of attention. In light of this evidence, the Taylor family disowned Pritchard entirely and public opinion turned against him. Stories of Pritchard's final weeping farewell to his wife as she lay in her coffin surfaced, and it was widely considered that Pritchard was crying 'crocodile tears' over his wife, originating from the myth that crocodiles would cry when eating their prey. This earned him the nickname 'The Human Crocodile'.

It was revealed in court that both Mary and her mother had known of Pritchard's affair with the servant girl, Mary McLeod. Furthermore, a policy on his wife's life would give Pritchard an annual income of £2,500. In his summing up, the judge stated that while Mary McLeod may have been involved in the administering of the poison, in his view she had no knowledge of what was taking place. The jurors required only an hour to deliberate, before delivering a unanimous 'Guilty' verdict to both counts. Lord Inglis sentenced Pritchard to death by hanging, just 21 days later.

During this time, Pritchard, like most condemned men, had a number of changes of heart. He took to reading the bible extensively, and made a number of contradictory confessions, at one point trying to clear his name and evade death by implicating Mary McLeod in the murders. Eventually he retracted the statement, absolving young Mary of all blame by saying: 'The sentence is just. I am guilty of the deaths of my mother-in-law and wife. I can assign no motive beyond terrible madness. I alone – not Mary McLeod – poisoned my wife.' The revelations of Dr Pritchard's woman-ising ways earned him a second nickname – the 'Poisoning Philanderer'.

At 8 a.m. on 25 July 1865, Dr Edward William Pritchard was taken to the gallows at Jail Square, besides Glasgow Green, for what was to be the final public execution in Scotland. About 100,000 people had come to watch the spectacle. This was mainly down to the infamy and the outrage that his trial provoked, but also in part down to his hangman, William Calcraft, widely known as the hangman *extraordinaire*, with the longest career and the shortest rope in the business. His use of the latter meant that his victims did not die quickly, as they would in the hands of a more competent executioner, but instead would strangle slowly to death. On occasions, Calcraft had been obliged to swing on the legs of the condemned man in an attempt to speed his end.

Ordinarily, executions by hanging would take place with a curtain placed below the floor of the scaffold, in order that the condemned could experience their last moment of suffering in private. However, the crimes committed by Pritchard were considered so heinous that the spectators were permitted to witness the whole process. At 8.10 a.m., a hood was placed over Pritchard's head, a brief prayer was said, and the executioner released the trap. Pritchard did not die quickly: his body was reported to have convulsed over a dozen times before death. However, we can be certain that Pritchard died a quicker and less painful death than his unfortunate victims.

THE FRENCH TUTOR

Date: 1878
Place: Edinburgh

THE FRENCH TUTOR

When Eugène Marie Chantrelle arrived in Edinburgh in 1866, he had little difficulty establishing himself as a well-respected member of society. At the age of thirty-four, he was a handsome, cultured Frenchman and an excellent linguist, who soon found work in some of the leading academic institutions in the city. Not just an excellent teacher of French and German, he was proficient in Latin and Greek, which equipped him admirably for providing private tuition. Among his accomplishments was writing a number of French textbooks that were adopted by many schools.

Chantrelle's impeccable credentials masked what was already a colourful career. He was born in Nantes, the son of a wealthy ship-owner, who ensured that his son received an excellent education. In due course, he commenced studying at Nantes Medical School, where he excelled, but his education came to a halt with the revolution in France in 1848, for it was then that his father found himself in such reduced circumstances that the young Eugène was left to fend for himself. He made some attempt to continue training for a career in medicine by attending medical classes in Strasbourg and Paris, but failed to apply himself to the task, and his life began to drift aimlessly.

Chantrelle had become very influenced by Communism, and in 1852, at the age of seventeen, he was manning the barricades with his fellow Republicans in Paris at the time of the *coup d'état*, during which he received a sabre wound to his

arm. Ending on the losing side made it a prudent move for him
to leave Paris, and after drifting through France, he sailed for
America. He spent several largely undocumented years there,
before arriving in England in 1862, where in Newcastle and
then Leicester, his teaching ability started to come to the fore.

The darker side of Chantrelle's nature had been demonstrated quite soon after his arrival in Edinburgh. On 1 January
1867, Ellen Holme went to Chantrelle's home at 81 George
Street, in response to a newspaper advertisement for the position of housekeeper. Miss Holme, in her late twenties, had been
trying to find a position as a governess, without success, and her
circumstances forced her to seek alternatives. The interview
proceeded with little mention of the duties that were to be
undertaken, but Chantrelle offered a sympathetic ear to her
predicament. However, as they talked, he became increasingly
amorous, culminating in him throwing her to the dining-room
floor and raping her. She did not report the incident, and nine
months later, gave birth to his child in Cromer.

In the meantime, Chantrelle had secured further work teaching French at a private school called Newington Academy,
where amongst his pupils was the fifteen-year-old Elizabeth
Cullen Dyer, who soon became the object of his lust. So it was,
at the age of sixteen, and seven months pregnant, Elizabeth,
somewhat reluctantly, became his wife on 11 August 1868. It is
reasonable to assume that Chantrelle shared her lack of enthus-
iasm, and entered into the marriage to protect his reputation in
society as far as possible, for the cruelty that was to mark their
marriage commenced even before their first child was born two
months after they married.

Over the next ten years they had three more children,
although one died, and it was surely only the love for her
children that made her return to him after taking refuge with
her mother on so many occasions. An increasingly heavy
drinker, Chantrelle subjected his wife to mental and physical

cruelty, threatening to take her life by poisoning her, and on one occasion brandishing a loaded pistol. At least twice the police were called for her protection, and she consulted a lawyer regarding a divorce but did not proceed, yet still she returned to him again and again, despite his barely-concealed infidelities in the brothels of Edinburgh.

Their maid noted that Chantrelle's alcohol consumption had now reached a bottle of whisky a day, and bearing in mind that he spent little time there, no doubt he consumed considerably more in surroundings that he found more to his taste. Inevitably, his work began to suffer. Word of his drinking and loose morals had spread, and demand for his teaching services had declined, leaving him with increasing debts. By 1877 he had 17s 11d in the bank with debts of £200, and tradesmen were beginning to press. It was about this time that an accident involving his pistol turned his mind to the matter of insurance. After making discreet enquiries into the definition of accidental death with one insurance company, he then approached the Accidental Assurance Association of Scotland; he insured his wife for the sum of £1,000 against accidental death. Having lived in constant fear of harm for many years, Elizabeth commented to her mother that her life would soon be over, now that is was insured.

* * *

It was on New Year's Day 1878 that Elizabeth Chantrelle first felt unwell, and retired to bed early. The maid, Mary Byrne, had been given the day off, and when she returned at about ten o'clock that night, she found her mistress in bed with her youngest child beside her. Elizabeth told the maid that she was feeling ill, and asked for some lemonade and an orange. Having supplied these, the maid left her in the room with her child, and the gas burning. During the night she heard the youngest child being hushed by one of its siblings, and assumed the child had been returned to the other bedroom which was normally occupied by Chantrelle himself and the two older children.

It was some time after six o'clock the following morning that the maid got up and set about her daily duties, when she heard the sound of moaning coming from her mistress's bedroom. The door was open, and she found Mrs Chantrelle lying unconscious alone in bed, moaning loudly. The gas light had been turned out, and in her subsequent testimony the maid confirmed that she had detected no smell of gas. Hurriedly she called Chantrelle who, after standing at his wife's bedside for a few moments, despatched the maid to the other bedroom as he said he could hear the baby crying.

The maid did as she was told, but on finding the child asleep, returned to the other bedroom to find Chantrelle just moving away from the window. Shortly after, he asked if she could smell gas, to which she replied she could not, but soon after she began to smell it strongly, and hurriedly went to turn off the supply to the meter. In the meantime Chantrelle had dressed quickly, and returned with a local doctor, Dr Carmichael, who in turn sent word for Dr Littlejohn, the medical officer of Edinburgh, but only after having moved Mrs Chantrelle to the other bedroom in view of the strong smell of gas that still pervaded her room. Cases of coal-gas poisoning were still rare, so Dr Carmichael was eager to have the vastly more experienced Dr Littlejohn present. Mrs Chantrelle's mother was called to the house, and with her agreement her daughter was moved to the Royal Infirmary, where a further examination of the patient was carried out by Professor Maclagan. His conclusion was that the symptoms were not consistent with those of coal-gas poisoning, but rather with those of narcotic poisoning. Their deliberations were irrelevant to Mrs Chantrelle, who died that afternoon without regaining consciousness.

When Professor Maclagan and Dr Littlejohn carried out the post-mortem the following day, it was inconclusive. It confirmed their belief that death was not due to coal-gas, but failed to find any trace of narcotic poisoning or any other definable cause of death. Because of the speed of absorption of poison, their findings did not rule out its use, but neither did they confirm it. However, further investigations proved more fruitful. The dead woman's nightdress and bed clothes had been retained, and further medical experts were called in to analyse the stains on them from where Mrs Chantrelle had vomited. This provided clear evidence of the presence of opium.

At his wife's funeral on 5 January 1878, Chantrelle gave an emotional display, including trying to throw himself into the open grave, but immediately afterwards he was arrested for her murder by the administering of opium to her orange and lemonade.

If Chantrelle's arrest was prompt, his trial was less so. It took some four months for the case to reach court, in the course of which 115 witnesses were assembled, and numerous statements taken to document the long history of threats and abuse in the marriage. Police investigations had proved fruitful. On searching a locked cupboard in Chantrelle's classroom, they discovered a collection of homeopathic drugs together with various poisons, including arsenic. They established that on 25 November 1877, Chantrelle had purchased sufficient extract of opium to kill thirty people, but could find no trace of the poison in the collection they had found.

In his statements leading up to the trial, Chantrelle stated that the friction in his marriage was due to his wife having been unfaithful to him twice, for which he forgave her. Also he alluded to her suicidal tendencies, and her consumption of chloral, used as a tranquilliser which aided sleep.

The case had received extensive press coverage, so when the trial started on Tuesday 7 May 1878, a huge crowd had braved the elements to congregate in Parliament Square in the hope of gaining admission to the court proceedings. The prosecution was led by the Lord Advocate and the Solicitor-General, aided by two deputy advocates, while Chantrelle's defence was in the hands of John Trayner and two assistants.

Chantrelle entered the court looking pale and rather weary, but nevertheless calm, and entered his 'Not Guilty' plea in a clear and steady voice.

The prosecution case discounted the theory of suicide, demonstrated by the fact that witnesses had confirmed Mrs Chantrelle to have been in good spirits on the day before her death. They pointed out that although the use of opium had not been confirmed by the post-mortem, the analysis of the bed clothes and nightdress had confirmed its presence. Chantrelle was well versed in matters relating to poisons, and was known to have purchased the opium. Furthermore, he had attempted to conceal the means of his wife's death by causing a gas leak. The gas pipe behind the shutter in his wife's bedroom had been fractured in a way that could not have been accidental, and although the accused had claimed to be ignorant of the presence of the gas-pipe, witnesses confirmed he had been present when the same pipe was being repaired some time previously. The fracture to the pipe was such that the escape of gas was considerable, yet the maid had not been able to detect it on her initial entry into the room, and had only been able to do so after leaving Chantrelle alone in the room for a short period. It was proposed that he had been the last person to visit his wife that night, and had given her the deadly lemonade and orange. His motives were clear – the long history of threats, his parlous financial position and the recent insurance policy.

Mr Trayner for the defence was limited in what he could achieve. Not seeking to explain the death of Mrs Chantrelle in any way, he concentrated on the key point of the defence, namely that no trace of the poison was found in the dead woman's body, that her symptoms were not consistent with those of opium poisoning and that the remainder of the evidence was purely circumstantial. Throughout the trial Chantrelle had remained calm, following proceedings closely but seemingly undisturbed by them. However, on the final day, he seemed surprised by the relatively short closing summary by Mr Trayner, and was heard to ask repeatedly, 'Is that all the evidence for the defence?'

At five minutes past four on the afternoon of Friday 10 May, the jury retired. Within an hour they had returned, with a unanimous vote of 'Guilty'. Chantrelle had remained calm throughout this, but when the Lord Justice Clerk passed the death sentence, he snapped, loudly asserting that the evidence had not established whether his wife had taken the opium herself, or whether some other person had done so; that the opium found on the bedclothes had been rubbed there by someone seeking to incriminate him. His acknowledgement of opium being the cause of death rather served to undercut one of the main assumptions of his defence.

The verdict was a popular one with the crowd waiting outside the court, and a chorus of abuse met Chantrelle when he was led to the prison van. Unlike some described in this book, the trial had been fairly conducted throughout, the evidence well-presented and the judge's closing comments to the jury were impartial and well explained. Despite this, certain rumours began to circulate: that two of the jury were asleep during the judge's summing up and a third suffered a condition that made him unable to assimilate written evidence. The matter was taken sufficiently seriously for the Lord Justice Clerk to refute the allegations at a sitting of the High Court of the Justiciary.

The date of execution was set for Friday 31 May. It was to be a first in Scottish legal history, as the Capital Punish-

ment Amendment Act of 1868 had stipulated that executions should now take place in private within the prison
walls, unlike the last in Edinburgh, the public hanging of
George Bryce thirteen years before. Chantrelle remained
cool and indifferent in prison; resistant to the ministrations of
a Roman Catholic priest, he gave a warmer reception to the
local parish priest, who visited him many times. Just occasionally his resolve would fail; one of his warders heard him
pronounce, 'Would that I could but place a fuse in the centre
of this earth, that I could blow it to pieces and with it all of
humanity! I hate them.'

Chantrelle passed the time by drawing up a statement of his
views on the case. It reiterated that the evidence against him
was purely circumstantial; no trace was found of opium in the
body, and as far as the stains containing the opium were
concerned, it had not been established that they had emanated
from the deceased. A petition was raised and well supported,
its content restating the element of doubt surrounding the
verdict, and requesting the sentence be commuted to one of
life imprisonment. Various meetings were held, primarily by
opponents of capital punishment, and the petition submitted
to the Home Secretary.

Chantrelle followed the progress of the petition closely, his
spirits buoyed by the prospect of a commutation, but at eight
o'clock on the morning before the day of his execution, he
learned that the request had been declined. Many of his final
hours were spent with the parish priest, which seemed to bring
him some comfort, and he remained composed throughout.
Woken at five o'clock on the morning of the execution, he
dressed and enjoyed a light breakfast and a last smoke. Finally,
as eight o'clock approached, the procession of legal and prison
officials proceeded to an outhouse, the floor of which acted as a
ceiling to a deep cellar below. Chantrelle stood upon the
trapdoor cool to the last, the rope placed around his neck, and

as the Reverend Wilson recited the Lord's Prayer, he took the eight-foot drop to oblivion.

After his death, a plaster cast of his head was taken for the Phrenological Museum, where it could be studied for evidence in support of the, then fashionable, theory that the dimensions and contours of the human skull gave clues to the causes of criminal activities.

To the last, Chantrelle maintained his innocence of the murder of his wife.

DEATH ON GOATFELL

Date: 1889
Place: The Isle of Arran

Our next story begins, not in Scotland, but in the leafy suburbs of Tooting, south London, in 1889, for there lived Edwin Rose, a thirty-two-year-old bachelor, who worked as a clerk for a builder in Brixton. Edwin was a personable man, always smartly dressed, dark and slim, with a luxuriant moustache. His single status, coupled with the fact that he lived at home with his father, older brother and four sisters, meant that, apart from his expenditure on his wardrobe, he could save enough of his earnings to afford to go away for his summer holiday.

So it was, when July arrived, and he being a man who enjoyed physical activity, Edwin Rose caught the train to Scotland, prepared for a fortnight's walking through the highlands. He had packed his black leather Gladstone bag in a manner befitting an Englishman at leisure – apart from the inevitable tweeds, he took his chocolate and brown striped tennis jacket (and racket too, of course), and, amongst other things, a grey felt hat and white serge yachting cap.

His initial destination was the attractive seaside town of Rothesay, on the Isle of Bute, where he had booked accommodation at a rather splendid hotel called the Glenburn Hydropathic. There he met, as arranged, the Reverend Mr Goodman, the minister of a local Presbyterian church, who was a friend and also the son of his employer. Being a naturally affable and approachable character, it was not long into his stay before Rose had become friends with two visitors from Linlithgow, Francis Mickel and William Thom, who were also staying at the Glenburn Hydropathic.

A group of guests at the hotel had organised a party to visit the Isle of Arran, and so, on Friday 12 July, Rose and his companions boarded the Clyde steamer *Ivanhoe* when it docked at Rothesay on its way to Arran. Before long, Rose had struck up an acquaintance with a fellow passenger, a Scotsman in his mid-twenties whose visiting-card identified him as John Annandale. Annandale was dressed reasonably well, although clearly not having the same means as Rose, and was considerably less talkative, but they got on well, and agreed, on landing at Brodick, that they would share accommodation in the nearby village of Invercloy, and return the following day with their luggage. As it was Glasgow Fair week, accommodation was scarce, but eventually Annandale found the premises of Mrs Esther Walker, who offered him the use of a lie-to, essentially a small wooden out-house accessible only from outside, and with single bed. Annandale booked the 'room' for a week, commencing the following day, Saturday 13 July, and said a friend would be staying with him until Wednesday.

When they rejoined the steamer, Rose suggested Annandale accompany him back to the Glenburn Hydropathic, and there he was introduced to Rose's other friends, Mickel and Thom. As it happened, they too were planning to visit Brodick for the weekend, so the following day, the four men caught the *Ivanhoe* together. Over the weekend, they spent much time walking, boating, and dining together; Mickel and Thom had to return home on Monday afternoon, and Rose and Annandale announced their intention to climb Goatfell, the highest mountain on the island. Mickel had been disturbed by something about Annandale, who seemed reticent to reveal details about himself, and strongly urged Rose not to proceed with the climb. Rose said he would try to avoid it, but when they said farewell on the pier and Mickel and Thom boarded the *Ivanhoe*, they could not help but notice that Rose was dressed for climbing, in his tweed suit with matching hat, leather boots and leggings, a waterproof and a walking-stick. Rose and Annandale set off to climb Goatfell at about 3.30 p.m. that Monday afternoon, 15 July.

* * *

On Thursday 18 July, Edwin Rose's brother, Benjamin, waited at a railway station in London for his brother's arrival. When he failed to appear, his family became concerned, and telegraphed the Reverend Mr Goodman at the Glenburn Hydropathic, only to learn of Rose's trip to Arran with a friend, from which he had not returned. Days passed without further news, and so, on Saturday 27 July, Benjamin Rose arrived at Brodick with the Chief Constable of Bute. By then it had been established that Rose and his companion had been seen setting off together for Goatfell, and that Annandale had been seen catching the early steamer the following morning, alone.

It was on Sunday 28 July that the search for Edwin Rose began. Every day for the next week over two hundred men scoured the starkly beautiful mountains without success, until the evening of Sunday 4 August. One of the searchers, concentrating on the area around the east shoulder of Goatfell, climbed high on the mountainside, near a place called Coire-na-Fuhren – The Gulley of Fire – where he noticed a nauseating smell. This was soon traced to the vicinity of a large granite boulder lying in a gulley, and there, crammed beneath the boulder, and blocked in by over forty stones, held in place by pieces of turf and heather, was the body of Edwin Rose.

Nothing was touched until Dr Andrew Gilmour, a summer visitor from Linlithgow, had been summoned. Dr Gilmour found the body fully clothed, lying face down, the skirt of the jacket pulled back over the head. On the removal of the body

from under the boulder, Benjamin Rose was able to confirm
that it was his unfortunate brother. Dr Gilmour then undertook a detailed examination of the body. All the pockets were
empty, and one was pulled inside-out. Having lain there for
nearly three weeks, the body had begun to decompose, but
there was no mistaking the cause of the death. Dr Gilmour
found the whole face and the left side of the head 'fearfully
and terribly smashed'. There was a fracture to the top of
the left shoulder-blade, the highest vertebrae detached, and
there was damage to the ribs and left buttock. A search of
the surrounding area revealed various objects identified as
belonging to Rose strewn along the gully above where the
body was found. His walking-stick, a knife, a button, a pencil,
and a torn and trampled coat were found, and finally a tweed
cap, folded into four and partly hidden under a stone on the
bed of a small stream.

The following day, a post-mortem was carried out by Dr
Gilmour, and Dr Fullarton of Lamlash. Their conclusion was
clear – the blows had been inflicted by a heavy, blunt instrument. The hunt for John Annandale was on.

*   *   *

It is time to look more closely at the mysterious John Annandale, and the events that led him to be on Goatfell that day.
Francis Mickel's suspicions of his background were justified,
as John Annandale was an alias adopted by John Watson
Laurie, a pattern-maker working at the Atlas Automotive
Works in Springburn, and living in lodgings in Glasgow. He
came from a respectable family, but there was talk of a history
of theft, and he was not well thought of. Anxious to rise above
his modest social status, and being by nature rather secretive,
Laurie had already adopted his alias when he arrived on
holiday in Rothesay, and booked into the house of a Mrs
Currie for the next fortnight. On Friday 12 July, he told his

landlady he was going to Arran for a few days, and left carrying his clothes in a brown bag, boarding the *Ivanhoe* for his chance encounter with Edwin Rose.

By coincidence there was someone aboard the *Ivanhoe* that Laurie knew, James Aitken, a grain merchant from Glasgow, who had met Laurie (and knew him by that name) from meeting him in Rothesay the previous year. They engaged in a brief conversation during which Laurie pointed out Rose, and mentioned their plans to go to Arran together. It would prove to be an unfortunate encounter for Laurie.

On Tuesday 16 July, he returned to Mrs Currie's boarding-house, wearing a grey felt hat, and carrying a parcel, which proved to contain a chocolate and brown striped tennis jacket, and a white serge yachting hat, which he wore for the rest of his holiday. He told Mrs Currie how much he had enjoyed his visit to Arran, and how he had climbed Goatfell. He requested her to have his bill and dinner ready for him for lunchtime on Saturday, but left that morning without paying, leaving behind various articles later identified as belonging to Rose. Later that day he bumped into James Aitken again. They chatted about Laurie's trip with his friend to Arran, and Aitken could not help but notice that the yachting cap that Laurie was wearing was remarkably similar to the one he had last seen being worn by Edwin Rose.

Laurie returned to his lodgings in Glasgow, and started his old life up again, but he had an unpleasant surprise when he encountered James Aitken for a third time on 31 July. By this time, the newspaper coverage of Rose's disappearance was widespread, so Aitken, remembering that Rose was the name of Laurie's travelling companion, and the familiarity of Laurie's headgear, promptly quizzed him on what he knew of 'The Arran Affair'. Laurie blustered that it was a coincidence, and that his friend Rose had returned to Leeds, then made a hasty excuse, promising to meet Aitken later. He never did, and when Rose's body was found four days later, Aitken took his story to the police.

In the intervening period, Laurie, realising that Glasgow was no longer safe, had taken prompt action. He left his job after being païd his wages to date and selling his pattern-maker's tools, abandoned his lodgings, although, surprisingly, he sent his landlady the rent that was due. By 6 August he was in Liverpool, renting a room for a week in advance, only to leave two days later, probably after seeing the true identity of 'John Annandale' revealed in the *Liverpool Courier*. As the hunt for him intensified, he wrote a letter to the *North British Daily Mail* denying any responsibility for Rose's death, saying he had left him in the company of two men on Goatfell, and seeming to hint that he might commit suicide. A second letter, dated 27 August, and postmarked Aberdeen, repeated his protestations of innocence. By this time, police had located his former lodgings in Liverpool, and recovered a box containing more articles belonging to Rose. On 4 September, as he was buying a ticket for a train, he was spotted by a police constable, and, following a lengthy pursuit, was found under a bush, an open razor at his side, and a superficial cut to his throat. The game was up. As he was cautioned, he said 'I robbed the man, but I did not murder him.' The following day, on being returned to Rothesay, he was charged with the murder of Edwin Robert Rose.

* * *

The trial commenced on Friday 8 November 1889 at the High Court of the Justiciary in Edinburgh. Such was the interest in the case, generated by the dramatic circumstances of the murder, and the lengthy pursuit of the prime suspect, that a crowd of about two thousand people was jostling around the entrance to the court when proceedings started at 10.00 a.m., under the watchful eye of the Lord Justice Clerk, Lord Kingsburgh.

A curious feature of both the prosecution and defence cases was that each ignored the more obvious explanation of events from their respective points of view. The prosecution's case was based on the premise that Laurie had lured Rose down to the place where his body was found, striking him with a rock on the left side of the head from above and behind as they descended the slope, then bludgeoning him around the head and face to hinder identification, before looting the body, and concealing it carefully under the boulder where it was found. No particular explanation was offered as to why Laurie, having taken so much trouble with concealment, had not hidden Rose's possessions that were left strewn down the hillside. If Laurie had set off on the journey with murderous intent, then surely a well-timed shove in the back at some hazardous stage in their climb would have been far easier than the method suggested.

From the defence point of view, an obvious explanation would have been that Rose had slipped and fallen to his death, the injuries being a result of the fall, and that Laurie had succumbed to temptation, looted the body, and subsequently stolen his luggage, making him a thief rather than a murderer. However, on Laurie's insistence, they proposed that he had left Rose on Goatfell with two men, and that he knew nothing of the concealment of the body, his only crime being the theft of Rose's possessions from their accommodation.

The central point of contention between the prosecution and the defence was over the cause of death. Sir Henry Little-john stated in evidence that he agreed with the conclusion of the doctors present when the body was discovered, and that the injuries were caused by a violent assault. He concluded that if the victim had fallen, as the defence suggested, then there would have been damage to the internal organs, which had proved not to be the case.

The medical experts for the defence had not had the opport-unity to examine the body, so their conclusions could only be theoretical. Dr Heron Watson felt that the injuries were more consistent with a fall, than with an assault. He described to the court his experimental attempts to smash a human skull, and his difficulty in inflicting the level of damage seen in the current case. He believed that Rose had slipped and fallen headlong over a cliff, smashing his skull on a boulder during his descent.

During the course of the trial various witnesses were called who had seen Laurie and Rose during their ascent of Goatfell. They were last spotted at about 6.25 p.m., high on Goatfell, and appeared to be discussing the best route down. It was another four hours before Laurie was seen again, walking in the direction of Corrie, and, shortly afterwards, buying a drink at the Corrie Hotel. It was calculated that to walk from where Laurie and Rose were last seen, to the Corrie Hotel, would take about an hour and forty minutes walking at normal speed, which raised the question, what had Laurie been doing for the rest of the time?

Having left his accommodation without paying, he was seen the following morning carrying two bags on his way to meet the boat. The description of one of the bags matched with that last seen in the possession of Edwin Rose. However, none of the items that Rose was known to have had about his person during the ascent of Goatfell, such as his watch and chain and pocketbook, were found in Laurie's possession.

When the prosecution summed up, they pointed out Laurie's use of a false name, the fact that he was the last man to be seen in the company of the dead man, and the undoubted theft of the dead man's possessions. All these facts combined made it clear, they concluded, that Laurie was the man responsible for the murderous attack, with theft as the motive.

When the defence addressed the jury, they stated that the prosecution had failed to establish beyond reasonable doubt whether a murder had actually been committed. They pointed out that there were no signs of a struggle having taken place, and that the injuries, being to the left-hand side of the body, were not consistent with an attack by a right-handed man such as Laurie, but that they were more likely to have been caused by a fall, in the way that the defence had already suggested. Furthermore, the accused was using an alias long before meeting the murdered man, and his conduct, fleeing only when his false identity was discovered, was more consistent with that of a thief than a murderer.

The Lord Justice Clerk, in his final summing up for the jury, stated that it was their duty to weigh the evidence and decide if it was sufficient to prove that Laurie was guilty of murder. At 9.45 in the evening of the second day of the trial, the jury retired to consider its verdict. Forty minutes later they returned, and the foreman announced a verdict of 'Guilty, by a majority'. In fact, the majority had been only one, eight voting for 'Guilty', and seven voting for that uniquely Scottish verdict 'Not Proven'.

Laurie stood as the Lord Justice Clerk pronounced the death sentence, and turning to face the benches said in a clear voice, 'Ladies and gentlemen, I am innocent of this charge.'

The prisoner was transported to Greenock, to await his execution on 30 November. However, a petition was raised by Laurie's family based on the fact that there was a history of insanity in the family, and that he had shown symptoms of this from an early age, which would go some way to explain his strange behaviour during the events which had recently taken place. Following an examination, the Medical Commission concluded that Laurie was of unsound mind, and two days before the scheduled date for his execution, the death sentence was commuted to penal servitude for life, and he was sent to Perth Penitentiary.

That was not quite the last that the public heard of John Watson Laurie. On being moved to Peterhead Convict Prison in 1893, he managed to escape from a working party in thick fog, but was overtaken by a warder on a bicycle. In 1909, after serving twenty years of his sentence, there seemed to be a prospect of parole, but instead he was moved to Perth criminal asylum, where he died in 1930 at the age of 69.

He never confessed to the murder, and so took to his grave the secret of what really happened that misty day on Goatfell.

THE MYSTERY OF ARDLAMONT

Date: 1893
Place: Argyll

In December 1893, one of the most sensational trials of the 19th century took place. Alfred Monson, a well-connected gentleman in his early thirties, stood trial for the murder of Windsor Dudley Cecil Hambrough, in the woods at Ardlamont House on 12 August 1893.

Cecil Hambrough was the son of Major Dudley Hambrough, grandson of John Hambrough, a famous botanist, and great-grandson of John Hambrough, a land proprietor who built Steephill Castle on the Isle of Wight. The family banking business, Hambrough Brothers of London and New York, was extremely prosperous, and the twenty-year-old Cecil stood in line to inherit a sum estimated at around quarter of a million pounds on reaching his twenty-first birthday.

Alfred John Monson was in his early thirties at the time of Hambrough's death. He, too, had impressive family connections, being the grandson of the late Earl of Galloway and the Honourable Reverend Thomas Monson, and nephew to Lord Oxenbridge, Master of the Horse for the Queen's Household. Monson had a privileged upbringing, having been educated at Rugby and Oxford. On completing his education, he found employment working for the government in South Africa, and it was in Cape Town that he met and married Agnes Maud Day, the daughter of a Yorkshire colliery owner, in 1881.

Becoming tired of their life in South Africa, he and his wife returned to England, where he found work as a tutor, another career which failed to hold his interest. He was perpetually short of money, and in the words of his wife, 'was prepared to sacrifice everything' in pursuit of greater wealth. In 1886, Monson was able to acquire the lease of a large mansion, Cheyney Court, which he insured against fire; fortuitously for his finances, the property was destroyed in a fire shortly after the policy came into effect.

In 1889, Monson made the acquaintance of Major Dudley Hambrough, Cecil's father, via a mutual friend and financier named Tottenham. Dudley Hambrough had run into financial difficulties and mortgaged his life interest to a company called Eagle Insurance Company. At this time, a life interest was the right to enjoy the use and benefit of another's land for the lifetime of the beneficiary. After mortgaging his life interest, Hambrough then failed to pay the interest due on the mortgage, thus making the insurance company full owners of his life interest.

Tottenham undertook to support the family finances, with a view to eventually buying the foreclosed mortgage from Eagle Insurance Company and taking over the Hambrough estates for his own use. Dudley Hambrough was determined that his son, Cecil, would join the army, and shortly after their first meeting, it was agreed that Cecil would live with Monson, who would be employed as his army tutor. The rate of £300 a year was agreed, payable upon the recovery of Major Dudley's finances. Given Monson's greed, it seems surprising that he was happy with this arrangement, so it seems likely that Tottenham was covering these expenses. Monson had identified the same opportunity as Tottenham and became obsessed with obtaining control of the massive Hambrough estate.

Monson found himself in court during 1890, when he was accused of fraud relating to a bill of sale. After a short trial he was acquitted, and quickly resumed his normal lifestyle – entertaining beyond his means, wildly overspending, and significantly overdrawing all his bank accounts. The Monson family, accompanied by Cecil Hambrough, moved on a number of times. Mrs Monson spoke little of the marriage, but at one time described their home life as unbearable. Monson was a very heavy drinker, with a high tolerance of alcohol: strong spirits seemed to have little effect on him. He entertained often and there was much drinking and revelry. Cecil Hambrough was very much under the control of Monson and trusted him completely. This became clear when there was a falling out between Major Dudley Hambrough and Monson. The Major was keen to enrol Cecil into the Hampshire Militia, where a number of the Hambrough family were already enlisted. He was furious to discover that Monson had already enrolled his son into the Yorkshire Militia, and he implored Cecil to leave Monson and return home; Cecil refused. Some angry letters were exchanged by Monson and the Major, but to no avail – Cecil Hambrough remained with the Monson family.

In the summer of 1893, Monson moved his family to Ardlamont House. Monson was bankrupt, and his plan to buy the life interest of Major Dudley had failed totally. The family were once again struggling for money, and Mrs Monson filed a claim for living expenses of £800 against Cecil Hambrough. Tottenham, who was still hopeful of purchasing the life interest in the family estate, continued to support the living expenses of the Hambroughs, and purchased the debt for £240.

Gaining the lease of Ardlamont House required some ingenuity on the part of Monson. Being bankrupt, and with Cecil still considered a minor, neither of them was eligible to sign the lease. However, Monson came up with a 'trustee and guardian' of Cecil, and the lease was granted, apparently co-signed by the trustee, Adolphus Frederick James Jerningham, another acquaintance of Tottenham. Jerningham later testified in court that he had been asked by Monson to be 'a kind of trustee for young Hambrough' but that this was his sole title to the office and he had heard nothing further about it; he had never seen the lease, and certainly had never signed it. On the signing of the lease, Monson had set about employing a suitable household staff, including a butler, cook, servants, gardeners and gamekeepers.

Monson's next move was to persuade young Cecil to take out two separate insurance policies on his own life, in favour of Mrs Monson. When Cecil, logically, questioned why, Monson explained that these were merely to secure advances made, and liabilities covered by the Monsons relating to the Hambrough Estates. Monson made a number of attempts to arrange the two policies on Cecil's life, initially approaching the Scottish Provident Institution and requesting cover of £50,000. Unsurprisingly, these were declined. Monson tried again, this time for £26,000 apiece. Again, these were declined. Eventually, Monson approached the Mutual Assurance Company of New York at their office in Glasgow. Now inventing a totally different story, Monson claimed he was the legal guardian of Hambrough, who was coming into an inheritance of £200,000 on his twenty-first birthday, and would be purchasing the Hambrough estates in his own name. Monson claimed that, in view of the short period before Hambrough received his inheritance, Mrs Monson was putting down a deposit of £20,000 for on-going expenses, which would be repayable upon payment of his inheritance. The life insurance policies were to cover her against any loss, in the unlikely event that Cecil Hambrough should die prior to this transaction.

Surprisingly, the insurance company did not check the story, or carry out any investigations into Mrs Monson's financial situation. Had they done so, they might have taken a very different view. Given that all incoming monies to Mrs Monson's account to date totalled a grand sum of £15, it is difficult to see how she would have honoured a cheque of £20,000.

However, the insurance policies were agreed, which Cecil Hambrough duly signed. He followed this up with a letter, dated 7 August 1893 and addressed to Mrs Monson, agreeing that if she were to agree to pay the premiums, she would hold the policies as security for all monies due from Hambrough to her. In the event of his death prior to repayment of these monies, she would be the sole beneficiary of the policies. Three days later, Cecil Hambrough was dead.

On 8 August 1893, a man named Edward Scott joined the family at Ardlamont House. He was not previously known to any of the residents. He was described by Mrs Monson as 'quiet and delicate-looking', and his accent marked him out as a Londoner. Monson said he was an engineer who had come to overhaul the boiler of the steam yacht that he had agreed to purchase. He joined the family for dinner that night, Cecil being absent fishing.

Earlier in the year, Monson had hired a rowing-boat for the season, but on the morning of the 9th, he asked the estate joiner if he could borrow his boat for a couple of days, as his existing one was not safe. Permission was given, and the boat moved to Ardlamont Bay. After lunch, Monson and Scott took Monson's children for a row around the bay, but, curiously, they took Monson's existing boat, which he had previously declared as being unsafe. On completing the trip, Monson and the children returned to the house, leaving Scott alone in the boat. After twenty minutes, he took off his shoes and socks and waded ashore.

Over dinner, a fishing trip was suggested, and about ten o'clock that night, Cecil Hambrough and Monson rowed out into the bay, once again using the 'unsafe' boat, leaving Scott on shore, next to the boat Monson had borrowed earlier in the day. Monson was a strong swimmer, but Cecil was unable to swim a stroke, so any accident in the water would be extremely dangerous for him. Monson's subsequent testimony stated that he and Hambrough had taken out the boat, which then struck a rock and capsized. Whatever the cause, both men were thrown overboard, but Monson resurfaced to see Hambrough sitting on a large rock. He swam to him and told Hambrough that he would swim to shore and bring the other boat out to collect him, knowing he could not swim.

He claimed he saw Scott when he swam ashore and ordered him to run to the house and fetch a lamp, to enable him to ensure that the rescue boat was fully safe. Then, rather than wait for Scott's return, he claimed he took a chance and took the boat out to rescue Hambrough. According to Monson's testimony, the three men then returned to the house where they shared drinks to toast their good fortune, before retiring to bed.

The next day, the owners of the two boats learned of the mishap, and headed to the beach to check on the damage to their boats. The original boat was found overturned on the shore, and the two gentlemen closely inspected the damage. The boat that had allegedly hit a rock and capsized showed no sign of damage, but they found a hole, about an inch and a half in diameter, had been cut out of the side of the boat. It was an odd shape, and had obviously been made with a knife. A knife was found inside the boat, the ownership of which was not established.

A later interpretation of the events of the previous evening was that the mysterious Scott and Monson had planned the murder of Cecil by drowning. Scott had cut the hole during the twenty minutes he was left by himself in the boat that afternoon, and the whole was concealed by fishing nets when Monson and Hambrough set off on their fishing trip. However, the hole was too large, and the boat shipped too much water; this resulted in the occupants taking to the water while still relatively near the shore, and Monson being forced to undertake an impromptu rescue mission.

The residents of Ardlamont House enjoyed a massive
640-acre estate in a spectacularly beautiful part of the Argyll-
shire countryside. The day following the boating accident,
10 August 1893, Monson invited his young pupil for a morning in the woods shooting rabbits. They were accompanied by
Edward Scott. Monson and Hambrough both carried guns,
while Scott was empty-handed; his role was to bag anything
that Monson and Hambrough managed to shoot. The three
men headed off into the woods. On their way, James Dunn,
who was holidaying in the area, witnessed them. He recognised Monson and Hambrough, but confirmed that he did
not recognise the third member of the party. He watched
them walk into the woods, where the party split up. Scott and
Monson branched off to the left, while Hambrough turned to
the right, alone.

Approximately three minutes later, Dunn reported hearing a
shot fired, which was also heard by a number of the workers on
the estate. Given that the men had gone out hunting, this was
to be expected. More unexpected was the fact that moments
later, Monson and Scott were seen by a ploughman leaving
the woods with the two guns. They passed without speaking
to him, but returned ten minutes later without the guns, and
told him that Hambrough had shot himself. Shortly after, the
butler found Monson and Scott in the dining-room and was
advised of the death; the three of them set out for the woods,
accompanied by other staff members. Cecil was discovered on
his back, next to a four-foot fence with a bullet hole behind his
ear. They wrapped the body in a rug, and transported it back to
the house on a farm cart.

It was assumed to be a tragic accident. A local doctor
was called, who examined the body, then joined the residents for
lunch. Scott mentioned that he had urgent business in Glasgow,
and would be catching the afternoon steamer; he duly did, and
promptly disappeared. Monson telegraphed to Tottenham to

notify him that Cecil had been involved in a serious gun accident and to come immediately. He also wired to the Hambrough family doctor, who told the Hambroughs. Major and Mrs Hambrough left immediately for Ardlamont – and not knowing that Cecil was in fact dead, instructed Monson to wire to Newcastle with an update as to his condition. No telegram awaited them at Newcastle, and the first Major Hambrough learned of his son's death was in an evening newspaper.

The Hambroughs arrived at Ardlamont on 12 August 1893, and were met by Monson. Major Hambrough asked to be taken to the place of Cecil's death. Monson obliged, taking him into the woods and pointing out the spot that Cecil had fallen. Major Hambrough remarked that it did not appear that a body had fallen there recently – there was a great deal of bracken and twigs that remained unbroken – surprising, as Cecil was a heavily-built lad standing at around six feet tall.

Monson accompanied the Hambroughs back home to Ventnor on the Isle of Wight, where their son was buried on 17 August. Monson returned to Scotland, and on 21 August visited the district manager of the Mutual, accompanied by the financier, Tottenham, to discuss the insurance claim. Apart from the death certificate, the insurance company required, as a formality, confirmation of the circumstances of the death from the Procurator Fiscal's office. However, when that office became aware of the two life insurance policies that had been taken out on Cecil's life, they started to look at the case in a new light. They recommended that Cecil's body be subject to a post-mortem, which was carried out on 13 September 1893, and was attended by Major Hambrough. The findings revealed that Cecil had been shot from a distance of approximately nine feet away. A twelve-bore gun had inflicted the wound, while Cecil's own gun was a twenty-bore. Monson had been carrying the twelve-bore; he was arrested for murder, with the absent Scott named as his accomplice.

A massive forensic investigation took place throughout the Ardlamont estate. Entire tree trunks from Ardlamont woods were submitted as evidence, and a whole host of ballistics and firearms experts stepped forward to offer their educated opinions. A further investigation into Monson's finances revealed that he had left behind a string of debts. He had hired a number of household staff, but had paid none of them. It came out, that during July, he had been in discussions with a Paisley shipbuilder, Mr Donald, to purchase a yacht for £1,200. Tellingly, he had advised Donald that he would purchase the yacht, but 'would be unable to forward a cheque until 10 August'.

The trial was set to start on 2 December 1893, and gained national coverage. The case was discussed at length, and the general opinion of the public was that Monson was clearly guilty. There were a huge number of witnesses for the prosecution – up to 110 witnesses appeared over the course of the trial: Ardlamont housekeeping staff, police officers, insurance company officials, doctors, solicitors and ballistic and firearms experts. One of the most famous witnesses in the courtroom was Dr Joseph Bell, a renowned Edinburgh surgeon and forensic detective, on whom Sir Arthur Conan Doyle based his master detective, Sherlock Holmes. Dr Bell told the courtroom that in his medical opinion, it was certain that Monson had murdered the young nobleman in the Ardlamont woods.

A number of stories were told to the court – along with inconsistencies in Monson's statement as compared to the forensic evidence, and details of Monson's sketchy financial history. Much evidence was shown to the court, including the various failed applications for life insurance in Hambrough's name, whole tree trunks from the Ardlamont estate, and even part of the boat, reflecting the plug hole that had been cut out in the previous attempt on Hambrough's life. A reward of £200 was offered for information leading to the arrest of the still-absent Scott.

Monson had hired John Comrie Thomson to defend him. Thomson was regarded as one of the most successful defence lawyers at the time; charismatic and believable, he set about defending Monson, primarily by picking holes in the case for the prosecution in an attempt to provoke doubt in the minds of the jurors as to Monson's guilt. Monson himself cut an impressive figure in court. He was slim, and more youthful-looking than his actual thirty-three years. Well groomed, he had neat blond hair, and a pale complexion. Visitors to the courtroom remarked on his 'strange shifty-looking eyes'. Monson remained calm and composed throughout the trial, maintaining an unruffled demeanour.

As the prosecution made their case against him, Monson seemed completely unflappable. Mary Cameron was one of the court artists employed, and she remarked that Monson had greeted her each day with a friendly smile, which she returned. After several days of the trial, she received a note from Monson, inviting her to tea in his cells during the customary afternoon interval. Mary refused, not because Monson was on trial for murder, but because they had not been formally introduced, and so it was not considered proper.

The trial continued for twelve days, when finally it was time for the summing-up remarks, and for the jury to consider their verdict. Thomson delivered a passionate speech, urging jurors to consider the verdict carefully. His closing statements remarked: 'We are all liable to make mistakes. I pray you make no mistake in this terrible matter. The result of your verdict is final, irreparable. What would any of you think if some day, it may be soon, this mystery is entirely unravelled and it is demonstrated that this man was innocent, while your verdict has sent him to his death?' The speech went on at considerable length, and the seed of doubt had been sown in the jurors' minds.

The jury retired to consider their verdict, and just 73 minutes later, returned with a verdict of 'Not Proven', a verdict unique to Scotland. These days forensic evidence would almost certainly have ensured Monson was convicted of Cecil Hambrough's murder, but in 1893, this small seed of doubt appeared to be all that was required; the jury, presumably, did not want the death of a man on their conscience.

Monson was duly freed to a minimum of fuss. When the verdict was delivered, friends of Monson cheered, the public clapped politely, and Monson disappeared quietly through a back exit to avoid the crowds. Tellingly, his defence counsel did not congratulate him, prompting suspicions that Thomson may not have believed as wholeheartedly in his client's innocence as it appeared in court. Undeterred, Monson wrote Thomson a letter of thanks for his closing statements in court, and expressed a wish to thank him in person soon. Thomson did reveal later that, during the trial, Monson was often so short of cash that he would hand over his cigar-cutter and watch as security for Thomson's work.

Ordinarily, after a case of this magnitude, it is usual for the protagonist to disappear from public view and make an effort to live a quieter and undisturbed life: Monson was no such character. In 1894, Madame Tussauds, deciding to profit from the sensational trial, erected a waxwork of Monson at the entrance to their Chamber of Horrors. Either Monson took exception, or, more likely, identified an opportunity to make some money, and sued Madame Tussauds for defamation. He won the case, but was awarded just one farthing in damages. This type of case was unprecedented at the time, and was used to establish the principle of 'libel by innuendo'. Monson vs. Tussauds became a well-known case in legal circles, and has been referred to when libel laws were being formulated in a number of countries.

Monson went free, but not for long. In 1896, he was soon up to his old tricks and was arrested and imprisoned for five years for fraud. Mrs Monson sued him for failure to support her and

her children. Monson counter-sued for divorce, citing Hambrough as the co-respondent.

   While Monson won his freedom, the Hambrough family
remained certain of his guilt and were enraged by the verdict.
For many years following his death, the family issued a notice
'In Memoriam' in the *Glasgow Herald*. Each year the message
read the same:

> *Sacred to the memory of Cecil Dudley Hambrough,*
> *shot in a wood near Ardlamont, August 10th, 1893.*
> *'Vengeance is mine, I will repay,' saith the Lord.*

THE TRIALS OF OSCAR SLATER

Date: 1908
Place: Glasgow

It was just after seven o'clock on a wet Monday evening three days before Christmas in 1908, and Nellie Lambie, a twenty-one-year-old servant, was hurrying through the damp Glasgow streets clutching a copy of the *Evening News*. Nellie was in the employment of Miss Marion Gilchrist, a rich old lady of eighty-three, who lived alone, apart from her servant, in a comfortable, well-appointed first floor flat.

The brief ten-minute excursion to buy the newspaper was a regular part of Nellie's daily routine, and despite her brief absence, she was always sure to close both the flat door and the external door of the block securely, as Miss Gilchrist was obsessive about security. The flat door had an impressive array of locks, chains and bolts, for she was not one to leave things to chance – perhaps for her personal security, or perhaps because of the jewellery worth an estimated £3,000 which she kept concealed in her wardrobe. Being prudent, Miss Gilchrist also had arranged with the occupiers of the flat below hers that she would knock three times on her floor should she be in need of assistance.

As Nellie climbed the stairs and approached the flat, she was surprised to see Mr Adams, the downstairs neighbour, poised with his finger on the bell. He explained that he had been at home when he heard what sounded like a fall, followed by three sharp knocks. Thinking it was Miss Gilchrist's signal, and encouraged by his sisters, he had rushed upstairs, noticing on his way that the front door to the flats was open, an unusual occurrence in itself. He had rung the bell three times without reply, although he could hear a noise that sounded like someone 'chopping sticks'. Assuming it was the servant working in the kitchen, he returned downstairs, but was urged to return by his sisters. On ringing the bell once more, the noise stopped, and he was pondering his next move when Nellie Lambie came up the stairs.

On hearing his story, she put the noise down to the pulleys in the kitchen, which were very noisy, but Mr Adams lingered on the step while she unlocked the two locks (the third was only used after they had retired for the night) and entered the hall, which was sizeable, with two doors on the left and right, but poorly lit by a gas mantle. As Nellie approached the kitchen door on the left, the bedroom door on the right opened, and out walked a man in a light overcoat. Arthur Adams had time to notice that he appeared to be a gentleman, who seemed about to talk to him, but instead stepped past him, and set off down the stairs like 'greased lightning'. Nellie checked the kitchen, reporting that all was well with the pulleys, then checked the bedroom before, urged by Adams, she entered the dining room. Her piercing scream bought him immediately to her side, and there, in front of the fireplace, lay Miss Gilchrist; a rug had been thrown over her head, but the amount of visible blood betrayed her fate. Arthur Adams wasted no time in scrambling down the stairs and out on to the street, rushing east, then west, but without sight of the fugitive.

On his return, he found that Nellie had attracted the attention of a policeman, so they returned to the dining room to examine Miss Gilchrist. On removing the rug, they saw that the old lady appeared to have been hit repeatedly around the head, but seemed to be still breathing. Adams hurried across the road, and returned with a doctor (coincidentally also called Adams). He confirmed that she was now dead, and identified the instrument of her demise as the blood-stained chair at her side.

When detectives arrived, a detailed examination of the flat was undertaken. In the spare bedroom a lamp had been lit, and a spent match, alongside a box of 'Runaway' matches, was found on a table. Nellie confirmed that the lamp had not been lit when she had departed, and that the matches did not belong in the house. On the same table was a watch and chain, some jewellery on a tray and a wooden dispatch box that had been forced open, the papers within scattered across the floor. Although some jewellery had been left untouched, including three rings and a gold bracelet, the maid was able to confirm that a diamond crescent brooch was missing.

The police asked Adams and Lambie for their description of the man they had seen leaving the flat. Both were a little uncertain – Nellie because the hall was poorly lit, and Arthur Adams because he had not been wearing his glasses. Their best endeavours resulted in this initial description put together by the police, and published in the following day's newspapers:

> A man between twenty-five and thirty years of age, 5 feet 8 or 9 inches in height, slim build, dark hair, clean-shaven; dressed in a light grey overcoat, and dark cloth cap. Cannot be further described.

That such a genteel old lady could be done to death violently in the safety of her own home caused uproar in the press, and the pressure on the police to provide a prompt resolution to the case was considerable. Their initial theory was that the murder had been done by someone known to Miss Gilchrist, as the untouched jewellery (and the three thousand pounds worth hidden around her bedroom) suggested that robbery was not the primary motive.

Their investigations received a boost when Mary Barrowman, a fourteen-year-old message girl, came forward two days after the murder to declare that she had seen a man emerge hurriedly from Miss Gilchrist's block of flats at about 7.10

on the fatal night. She was standing under a street light when
he brushed past her, and ran off down the road. The police
were rather perplexed to find that her description of the man
differed so much from that given by Adams and Lambie, that
they decided they were looking for two men in connection
with the crime.

Mary Barrowman's description of the second man resulted
in the following.

> The man wanted is about twenty-eight or thirty years of age,
> tall and thin, with his face shaved of all hair, while a distinctive
> feature is that his nose is slightly turned to one side. The
> witness thinks the twist is to the right side. He wore one of the
> popular round tweed hats known as Donegal hats, and a fawn-
> coloured overcoat, which might have been a waterproof, also
> dark trousers, and brown boots.

Both descriptions were published in the Glasgow evening
newspapers on Christmas Day 1908. On the same day, Chief
Constable Stevenson issued a Murder Notice for circulation
within the police force, which gave the official view of how the
two sightings took place.

> On her return with the paper the servant met the man *first*
> described leaving the house, and about the same time another
> man, *second* described, was seen descending the steps leading to
> the house, and running away.

Christmas Day also brought the first significant progress in
the investigation, when the police received a visit by Allan
McLean, a Glasgow bicycle dealer. McLean was a member of
the Sloper Club in India Street, a social club mainly devoted to
gambling. On reading the description of the stolen brooch in
the newspapers, he recalled that a member of the club, a
German Jew he knew only as Oscar, had been trying to sell a
pawn ticket for a diamond crescent brooch, and he wondered if
this might be the brooch the police were seeking. Although he
did not know Oscar's exact address, he recalled walking home

from the club one night, and noticing the building that Oscar had entered.

The police wasted no time in getting McLean to show them the address in question, a flat at 69 St George's Road, which was about 400 hundred yards from the late Miss Gilchrist's residence. The police raided the flat at midnight. A sign on the flat door said 'A. Anderson, Dentist', but on entering, the police found only a servant, Catherine Schmalz. The facts were soon established. The man who lived there was called Oscar Slater, a gambler and jewel dealer. He shared the flat with a lady known as Madame Junio, who was known to be his mistress, although it was believed he was not the only recipient of her affections. Police interest was aroused further when they heard that Slater and his mistress had departed that very day to Liverpool, with the intention of sailing on the liner *Lusitania* to New York. This was starting to sound very promising to the police – the culprit, having read the description of the 'second man' involved in the murder, which had been published for the first time that day, had promptly taken flight, and now they were in hot pursuit. The hunt for the killer of Marion Gilchrist was on.

* * *

Oscar Slater's real name was Oscar Joseph Leschziner. Born in Germany, he was the son of a Jewish baker, and spent his early working life as an apprentice to a timber merchant, and then as a bank clerk in Hamburg. With the prospect of military service looming, Oscar left the country, and headed for London. There began his association with gambling; initially a bookie's clerk, he became a bookmaker in his own right, and started to get involved in the running of gambling clubs. This took him around the country, then to the United States. In 1902 he was in Glasgow, and there he had married a local girl, May Curtis. The marriage soon went wrong in spectacular fashion, his wife proving to be an alcoholic and a compulsive spender. Although he soon left her, they did not divorce, and she spent the ensuing years pursuing him for money. When Slater had left Germany, he had decided he needed a more English name, and, as he later explained, to try to shake his wife off his trail, he adopted a variety of names – Anderson, Schmidt, George and Sandro amongst them – but it was as Oscar Slater that he was most commonly known.

Shortly after separating from his wife, he met Andrée Junio Antoine at the Empire Theatre in London. She became his companion for the next five years, as his business affairs took him to New York, where he became involved in the running of various clubs, before returning to London in autumn 1908. Slater travelled to Glasgow in late October, followed by Madame Junio and their servant a week after, and within a few days they had rented the flat at 69 St George's Road, and purchased some furniture on hire purchase. Also he purchased a set of household tools, which would become significant at a later date, then settled into a routine, circulating around pubs and gambling clubs looking up old friends, and dealing in a little jewellery.

Oscar Slater had a very distinctive appearance compared with the usual residents of Glasgow. Well-dressed and broad-shouldered, he had a prominent (but not twisted) nose and a small moustache, but his main characteristic was that he most definitely looked *foreign*.

The police case against their prime suspect then suffered an unexpected and, if logic had prevailed, terminal setback. It had proved a reasonably easy matter for the police to track down the pawn shop that issued the ticket that Slater had been attempting to sell, but they were disappointed to find that the brooch had been pawned on 18 November, some weeks before Miss Gilchrist's murder. If additional confirmation was needed, the servant Nellie Lambie was able to state that the brooch was definitely not the one formerly in the ownership of her mistress.

Effectively this had disposed of the one piece of evidence that linked Slater with the murder, and there was no good reason for the police to continue their pursuit, but continue they did, sending a message to detectives in New York requesting that they intercept Slater when he and his companion disembarked from the *Lusitania*. This decision was the key moment in the case, and raises the question of why it was taken. Under pressure to find the culprit, Slater was a perfect solution: operating on the fringes of society in slightly dubious company, known to deal in jewellery, and best of all *foreign* – explaining at a stroke how such a brutal murder could take place in such a respectable city.

When the *Lusitania* docked in New York on 2 January 1909, Slater and his companion were promptly arrested by the New York police. Because extradition proceedings would be required to facilitate Slater's return to Scotland, the Glasgow police decided to send all three of their witnesses, Lambie, Adams and Barrowman, across the Atlantic to New York to identify their quarry. To give the witnesses a little assistance, they thoughtfully showed them pictures of the 'suspect' they were taking such a long journey to identify, and they were well drilled in the role of appearing as identification witnesses. The day after their eventual arrival in New York on 25 January, Lambie and Barrowman were asked to sit in a corridor outside the Police Commissioner's office, when Oscar Slater was walked past them handcuffed to a U.S. Marshall, and both immediately recognised him.

When they appeared in the U.S. court, not surprisingly they had no difficulty in picking out Slater, although as far as linking him to the scene of the crime, Lambie said she had not seen his face at the scene of the crime, but recognised his walk. Barrowman said he was 'something' like the man she had seen. Arthur Adams said no more than that he 'resembled' the man. If Slater had taken the advice of his counsel and opposed the extradition proceedings, he would have stood a good chance of succeeding, in the face of the less than convincing testimony on offer, but he was adamant – he would return to Glasgow to clear his name.

* * *

Meanwhile, on the other side of the Atlantic, the Gilchrist murder and the pursuit of Oscar Slater was front-page news, and when his picture was published, in conjunction with a £200 reward, a flood of new witnesses came forward claiming to have seen him. The police selected twelve who claimed to have seen a suspicious stranger lurking outside Miss Gilchrist's block of flats for some weeks before the robbery. None knew Slater, and none commented on his foreign appearance. Their memories were assisted by being shown a picture of Slater, and when it came to the identity parade, the swarthy suspect was put in a line-up comprising nine policemen and two railway workers, all Scotsmen. Not surprisingly, the identification of Slater as 'the man' was a formality. His trial was scheduled for Monday 3 May 1909, at the High Court of Justiciary at Edinburgh.

Lord Guthrie was appointed as the judge, and the prosecution was undertaken by the Lord Advocate, Alexander Ure. There had been talk in legal circles that the crown were considering dropping the case because the evidence was so poor, but the Lord Advocate was determined to proceed. The preparation of the prosecution's case required some care, as the witness statements they had assembled were extremely variable, and in some cases contradictory. For instance, a young school teacher, Agnes Brown, had seen two men fleeing the scene of the crime, one dressed in a grey coat, the other in a blue overcoat with a velvet collar. The police thought that the description of the first man tallied sufficiently with that of the man seen by Adams, Lambie and Barrowman, and thus was Slater, and were extremely vexed when Miss Brown identified Slater as the second man. It was decided that her testimony would not be required. Another witness that the police decided they could do without was Arthur Adams's sister, Mrs Liddell, who had seen a man loitering outside the flats at five to seven on the night in question. Her description of someone wearing a tweed cap and a long tweed overcoat only added to the bewildering array of clothes that Slater was apparently seen wearing that night.

The prosecution's case came down to a procession of carefully selected witnesses, and the powers of persuasion of the Lord Advocate upon the jury. What the prosecution case did not prove, and indeed not even attempt to prove, was firstly, that Slater had prior knowledge of Miss Gilchrist's valuables (and indeed why the intruder had seemed more preoccupied with her papers than her jewellery) and secondly, the method by which he had entered the flat. This second point is particularly significant. To have opened both the outside door of the block of flats, and then the door of Miss Gilchrist's flat would have required the possession of two separate keys. The alternative was that the visitor had been admitted by Miss Gilchrist. If the bell had rung in Miss Gilchrist's flat, she was able to open the external front door by a handle within her flat. She could look out of her window to see the caller, or go out of her front door, cross the landing and look over the banisters to identify the visitor, which gave her ample time to retreat to the safety of her flat should she not care for the look of whoever she had admitted. It seems unlikely she would have been sufficiently taken by Slater's appearance to let him in on first acquaintance, so the inference was that she knew her killer. Indeed, the police had been working on this assumption at the start of the case, before it became incompatible with their pursuit of Oscar Slater.

Of the original three witnesses who had gone to America to identify Slater, Lambie and Barrowman were now certain in their testimony, indeed far more certain than they had been at the time of their original evidence, although they had, of course, been well coached in the intervening period. Lambie had actually changed her description of the clothes she had seen the man wearing, so they matched Barrowman's testimony, and now stated she had seen the man's face, whereas she had not in her statement in New York. Arthur Adams remained more constant, saying no more than Slater 'resembled' the man he had seen. One of the many witnesses who did not appear was Duncan MacBryne, who knew Slater by sight, and had seen him calmly standing at the door of his house at 8.15 p.m., barely an hour after he was supposed to have carried out the brutal murder.

Another interesting aspect of the prosecution's case was in connection with the murder weapon. The first medical man at the scene of the crime had been Dr Adams, who had identified the head injuries as having been inflicted by a heavy mahogany chair found next to the body. Strangely, Dr Adams took no part in the trial, as the police had come up with a different murder weapon. The set of household tools mentioned earlier as having been purchased by Slater contained a small hammer which the police found in his luggage in New York, and on which they identified some 'brown stains, together with a waterproof, also with some stains'. Professor Glaister, the chief medical expert for the Crown, who had carried out the post-mortem, testified that the hammer could have caused the grievous head injuries they had examined, assuming that the assailant had straddled the murdered woman and inflicted 20-40 rapid powerful blows. Dr Gault, the casualty surgeon, stated that he would have expected a heavier weapon and that 50 or 60 blows would have been required, probably more.

Slater's defence was conducted by Mr A. L. McLure, K.C., and concentrated heavily on the total lack of evidence to associate Slater with the crime scene in any way, and recounted previous cases where wrongful identification had caused wrongful convictions. Scientific experts for the defence had examined the hammer and waterproof, and had found nothing resembling blood stains. As far as Slater's movements on the night of the murder were concerned, he was known to have sent a telegraph regarding the repair of a watch, which was to have been ready by 30 December. Slater had heard that his wife was on his trail again for more money, so he was bringing forward his plan to travel to New York. He had spent some time at a billiard saloon, before leaving at 6.30 p.m., saying to a friend he was going home for dinner. He was dressed in a waterproof and a bowler hat, and the saloon was nowhere near Miss Gilchrist's flat. Madame Junio and the servant testified that he was home for dinner at 7.00 p.m. as usual. However, some damaging information did emerge. The Lord Advocate, cross-examining the servant, got her to admit that Madame Junio frequented music halls and entertained gentlemen in the evenings. Another witness stated that he had heard that Slater lived off his mistress's earnings. Slater was desperate to testify in his own defence, but his counsel refused to allow it, being concerned that his relatively poor, heavily accented English would turn the jury against him further.

It was the Lord Advocate's summing up to the jury that finally added some weight to the prosecution case. Speaking for two hours without notes, he glossed over the deficiencies of the prosecution case, or in some cases just changed the facts – a later analysis of his address identified twenty-five mistakes of fact or interpretation. Here was a man, he said, who lived off the earnings of prostitution – surely such a man would find robbery and violent murder of little consequence. It was a passionate and persuasive address.

The defence tried gamely to rebuff the prosecution's case with more reasoned arguments, but it fell upon the judge, Lord Guthrie, to issue guidance to the jury in his summing up.

He stated that the jury could have no doubt, having listened to evidence, that Slater 'had at least a marked resemblance' to the man seen at the scene of the crime. His lordship warmed to his main theme, that of the depraved life-style of the accused, whom he viewed as among the dregs of society. He concluded:

'The Lord Advocate founds on the prisoner's admittedly abandoned character as a point in support of the Crown. He is entitled to do so, because a man of that kind has not the presumption of innocence in his favour which is a form in the case of the ordinary man. Not only is every man presumed to be innocent, but the ordinary man, in a case of brutal ferocity like the present, has a strong presumption in his favour. In addition, a man with the prisoner's sinister record may be capable of exhibiting a callous behaviour even immediately after committing a murder.'

At 4.55 p.m. on Thursday 6 May, the jury retired to consider their verdict. Within an hour and ten minutes, they were back. Of the fifteen jurors, one had found Slater 'Not Guilty', five had voted for 'Not Proven', nine had voted 'Guilty'. The guilty verdict confirmed, and despite the prisoner's protestations of innocence, Lord Guthrie pronounced the sentence of death, the execution to take place in Glasgow on 27 May.

*　　*　　*

The day after the trial, a Glasgow newspaper strongly supported the verdict, for ridding society of a member of what they described as 'a brood of alien vampires', but the general public were less convinced. A public petition for the commutation of Slater's sentence, which raised 20,000 signatures, asserted a) that the identification evidence on which he was convicted was insufficient, and b) that the conclusion of the case was based solely on a judgement of his alleged immoral character. Following further submissions by Slater's legal team, the death sentence was commuted to penal servitude for life, and Slater was despatched to Peterhead, where he would spend the next eighteen and a half years of his life.

In April 1910 further interest in the case was aroused by the publication of *The Trial of Oscar Slater*, a detailed account of the court proceedings by the notable crimewriter William Roughead. Reviews of the book led to a flurry of correspondence being published in the English newspapers, a notable contributor being Sir Arthur Conan Doyle, who subsequently published a pamphlet on the case in 1912, suggesting that Miss Gilchrist's will, rather than her jewellery, might be the motive for her murder. Miss Gilchrist, it seems, was not on good terms with her relations, who seldom visited. By this time, questions were being asked in the House of Commons, but the Scottish Secretary declined to take further action.

While the public outcry continued, behind the scenes support for Slater was coming from a most unexpected source. In 1912 John Thomson Trench was a Detective-Lieutenant in the Glasgow police, and widely regarded as the best detective in Scotland at the time. He had been brought in to investigate what was known as the Broughty Ferry case, in Dundee, and certain aspects of the investigation reminded him strongly of the Slater case, with which he been involved, and provoked him to action. His account of the Slater case states that he knew that two detectives had interviewed Nellie Lambie on the night of the murder, and she had told them that the man she had seen leave the flat was known to both her and Miss Gilchrist. This supported the police theory at the start of the case that the victim knew her murderer. Then came the clue of the stolen brooch, and the pursuit of Oscar Slater, and Trench was instructed to drop the matter, but it had played upon his conscience ever since. He decided to put aside his duty as a policeman to maintain his silence over the affair, and he took his story to David Cook, a well-known Glasgow lawyer. Not wishing to risk his position within the police, agreement was reached that he would submit his evidence in confidence to the Scottish Secretary, Mr McKinnon Wood, who would guarantee that he would not suffer as a result of his disclosures.

The assertions made by Trench gave the Scottish Secretary little option but to set up an inquiry. Sir Arthur Conan Doyle greeted the news with the comment in the *Daily Mail*: 'The police are on trial as much as Slater. If the methods of the police are not to be investigated, the inquiry is futile.' This proved to be a very shrewd assessment.

The Sheriff of Lanarkshire was appointed to head the inquiry. It was to be held in secret, and neither the accused nor his legal representatives were permitted to attend. Witnesses were invited, but not obliged, to take part, and were not under oath. Their statements were not written down, but were summarised by the Sheriff, in his role as commissioner of the inquiry. It was also made clear by the commissioner that the inquiry 'should in no way relate to the conduct of the trial'.

Trench gave his account of how Lambie had confirmed her recognition of the man leaving the flat – known throughout the written account by the initials A. B. – to two detectives investigating the case. He described an interview with Margaret Birrell, Miss Gilchrist's niece, who had been visited by Nellie Lambie immediately after she had discovered the body, and who had told her she was sure that the man she saw was A.B. Miss Birrell said that the two detectives had confirmed to her that Lambie had said the same to them. Trench said he was aware that the two detectives had subsequently visited the house of A.B. but that he was unaware of the outcome, and that when he submitted his report to his Chief Superintendent, he was advised that the Superintendent of Western Police had decided that A.B. was not their man. Trench then went on to summarise the case, emphasising the lack of solid evidence, and casting doubt on whether Mary

Barrowman, one of the key witnesses, was in fact anywhere near the scene of the crime.

Faced by this betrayal by one of their own, the police presented a united front. One policeman after another testified to contradict Trench's account of the case. Miss Birrell and Nellie Lambie (now married) denied that the name of A.B. had ever been mentioned. The inquiry found no evidence to change Slater's sentence, and a transcript of the inquiry was eventually released as a white paper, notable for the copious use of asterisks to conceal significant parts of the testimonies recorded.

That Trench should have risked his career by making false allegations about the conduct of the case makes no sense, and the implications of the police actions seem clear. The promised protection of the Scottish Secretary for Trench counted for nothing. He was dismissed from the force, and joined the army, serving with the Royal Scots Fusiliers as a drill instructor. But the police had not quite finished with him. In May 1915, he and David Cook, the lawyer he consulted on the Slater case, were arrested in connection with matters relating to a jewellery theft in January 1914, some months before Trench's dismissal. The evidence presented by the police in support of the case was dubious, and the judge directed the jury to find Trench and Cook 'Not Guilty'. Trench continued his war service, and died in 1919, Cook two years later. Neither ever quite recovered from the effects of their trial.

*　*　*

So the years passed, Oscar Slater largely forgotten in the horror of the First World War and its aftermath. In normal circumstances a life sentence in Scotland equated to fifteen years imprisonment, at which time the prisoner would be released, but in Slater's case, perhaps because of his continued protestations of innocence, or perhaps because his release would raise the profile of his story once more, he remained behind bars. In 1925, Sir Arthur Conan Doyle received a message from Slater that had been smuggled out of Peterhead, beseeching him to try once more to effect his release, but once more Doyle's pleas fell on deaf ears.

It was not until 1927 that the case became the subject of national attention once more, with the publication of William Park's *The Truth About Oscar Slater*. Press coverage rocketed, and the *Daily News* retold the story of the trial over four issues. *The Empire News* responded by tracking down Nellie Lambie once more, who told how she recognised the man in the flat, but that the police had persuaded her she was wrong. She also recounted how Miss Gilchrist would be visited by a number of men, whom she would let in without the servant seeing them.

Not to be outdone, the *Daily News* located Mary Barrowman, who told how, during daily visits to the Procurator-Fiscal's office for a fortnight, her evidence was honed from saying that Slater was 'very like the man' to a definite identification.

Faced with this renewed uproar, the Scottish Secretary, now Sir John Gilmour, perceived the best course of action was to announce that Slater was now considered to have completed his sentence, and would be released forthwith. Faced with accusations in the press that this was simply a ploy to avoid a further inquiry, Gilmour agreed that Slater's case could be the subject of an enquiry by the Scottish Court of Criminal Appeal, which would be heard by five judges. Slater chose to view the proceedings from the public gallery. What he viewed was a great disappointment to him. Despite the fact that considerable time and effort had been taken to reassemble the witnesses that still survived, the judges stated that the purpose of the enquiry was to hear any new evidence that had come to light that would have affected the outcome of the original trial. After two days of legal debate, they specified which witnesses they were prepared to allow, but these did not include Slater himself, as they felt his evidence would represent no more than a repetition of his 'Not Guilty' plea.

Slater's first inclination was to give up on the appeal, but he was persuaded to continue. So it was that the appeal took place on 9 July 1928. The surviving witnesses appeared and gave their testimony, with the exception of Nellie Lambie, who declined to return from America. The judges then considered the case from four aspects, and on 20 July gave their unanimous verdict. On the first three counts: a) that the jury's verdict was unreasonable or unsupported by evidence, b) that any new facts had been disclosed material to the issue, and c) that the appellant had suffered prejudice by non-disclosure of evidence known to the Crown, they considered the appeal to have failed. However, the final point, that Slater was denied a presumption of innocence because of his perceived immorality, led them to state: 'In these circumstances we think the instructions given in the charge amounted to misdirections in law, and that the judgement of the Court before whom the appellant was convicted should be set aside.'

In the end, it was hardly the resounding 'Not Guilty 'verdict that Slater had hoped for. Had he sought proper representation at this stage, his claim for compensation could have been considerable, but as it was, the treasury offered him an *ex gratia* payment of £6,000, which he accepted. Financially secure, he left Glasgow, but remained in Scotland, marrying again, and living out his life in some contentment until his death in 1948 at the age of seventy-five.

In the many retellings of the case, most writers, including Conan Doyle, believe the mysterious A.B., a relative of Miss Gilchrist's, to be the killer. There is a story, which cannot be confirmed, that within the family the culprit was believed to be Austin Birrell. Whatever the truth may be, the killer was never found in this strange case, in which Miss Marion Gilchrist was not the only victim.

THE DALKEITH POISONER

Date: 1911
Place: Dalkeith

It was 3 February 1911, and Charles Hutchinson was finishing a lavish meal with a group of around eighteen friends. Charles, a well-connected freemason, was a wealthy man, who enjoyed entertaining, and was generous to his friends. The evening, arranged to celebrate the silver wedding of Charles and his wife, had consisted of several rounds of cards, followed by a late supper. Satisfied and full, the guests settled down to coffee, served by Charles's son John. Courteously, John served the women first, before moving on to the men.

Moments later, there was a commotion. A number of the women began to feel unwell, and almost immediately after, the gentlemen began to suffer from the same complaint. Charles Hutchinson and another guest, the local grocer Alec Clapperton, fell to the floor, screaming in agony and holding their stomachs. A number of guests stumbled out on to the front lawn, clutching their stomachs and vomiting. Other guests lay on sofas or on the floors, wailing in pain. Of the eighteen guests, only three were unaffected, including John Hutchinson. John carefully attended to the sick, seemingly trying to alleviate their suffering.

Two doctors were immediately called to the house, and tried valiantly to save Charles and Alec. Their efforts were unsuccessful; they were taken to hospital and died only hours later. A dozen of the remaining guests were all seriously ill, and were taken to hospital for treatment. In time, all the other guests recovered, including John's fiancée, who had also been stricken.

* * *

Charles Hutchinson was a well-regarded member of society, connected with the Duke of Buccleuch's estate office. He was well known throughout Dalkeith and respected among the circles he moved in. His son, John, was also well known but for very different reasons. Aged 24, John appeared to have gone off the rails in recent months. He had previously had a good job as a chemist, employed by his uncle's firm in Musselburgh, but suddenly had taken the decision to resign in order to speculate on the stock market. He claimed to have made a sum of £17,000 during the rubber boom, but many other investments in copper, oil and South African shares had proven unsuccessful.

Hutchinson had become notorious for his reckless lifestyle. Regardless of his lack of regular employment, he had just purchased a new car, and spent his days driving around the district. He took cruises to north Africa, and indulged in the current craze of roller-skating, a popular pastime in the capital. His extravagant spending soon caught up with him, and he began to accumulate substantial debts. By early 1911, he owed approximately £10,000, a significant sum for those times, and he had no means of repayment. Living with his parents, he owned no property or assets, except for his new car. Before long, bailiffs seized his car as part settlement of an account at an Edinburgh stockbroker. John's car was his pride and joy, and he was devastated when it was taken from him.

John's parents were busy planning their silver wedding. It is not known whether he had approached them for support and been refused, or if they had just not paid enough attention to understand how big his problems actually were. They may have been attempting to teach their son the value of money, and were not willing to immediately bail him out. Whatever the reason, John was not pleased and may have viewed the lack of interest as callous. Being engaged to be married at the time, he was most unhappy with his parents and their evident lack of concern.

In the meantime, Charles Hutchinson was looking forward to his and his wife's celebrations, keen to impress their friends with the finest quality food and refreshments. He bought fresh coffee from the local grocer, Clapperton, who was invited to attend the celebrations.

John was plotting ways to amass enough money to clear his debts, and fell upon the solution of his father's life insurance. In the event of Charles Hutchinson's death, his policy would pay out a significant sum of money to the family, more than enough to clear John's debts. Of course, the downside of this plan was that John would have to murder his father, but he decided that this was the only way out of his debts.

Stealing a bottle of arsenic from his uncle's dispensary, he used it to spike the coffee served at the dinner party.

* * *

The post-mortems on Charles Hutchinson and Alec Clapperton were carried out on Sunday 5 February 1911, and while, from the reported symptoms, the coroner suspected the cause to be arsenic poisoning, he had to await the results of chemical analysis of certain parts of the intestines for confirmation. In the meantime, the funerals took place. Charles Hutchinson's Masonic Lodge was well represented at the funeral, which over five hundred people attended, including some of the guests at the fateful silver wedding party. All those present could hardly fail to notice the abject grief displayed by John Hutchinson as he mourned his father's passing. He seemed devastated, and nobody who attended the ceremony at Esbank Cemetery had cause to suspect anything other than that his grief was genuine; they felt great sympathy for the young man, so clearly traumatised by the loss of his father.

On 10 February 1911, police confirmed that they had identified arsenic in the remains of the coffee that they had retrieved from the party. They had checked the milk used, and no arsenic was present. Initially suspecting Clapperton, despite the fact he was dead, police checked the supply of coffee in his shop, and discovered nothing untoward, thus concluding that the arsenic must have been added to the coffee between the time of the coffee being purchased and served at the party.

Naturally, suspicion then fell upon members of the Hutchinson household.

It transpired that, in order to poison all the members of the party, each individual cup of coffee would have had to be spiked, and it seemed unlikely that this could have been done by mistake. Initially, John Hutchinson was not considered a suspect, despite the testimony of many witnesses that he had served the coffee, as he gave the police no cause for suspicion when they interviewed him. His outward display of grief at the funeral may certainly have contributed, as well as the fact that his own fiancée had also been poisoned. The guests stricken with illness at the party could also testify to his seemingly genuine concern for the victims.

It was only when police realised that his previous occupation was a chemist that they decided to search John's belongings, before widening the search to his uncle's dispensary in Musselburgh. There, they discovered a bottle of arsenic to be missing, which could not be accounted for in the cash register, and appeared never to have been sold. Suddenly, the police had a prime suspect.

At this point, John Hutchinson fled. Suspecting rightly that the police would shortly put two and two together, he disappeared on 14 February, claiming that he intended to visit friends in Newcastle. This was, he said, to help clear his head and give himself a well-earned rest. He was expected back on 16 February, but failed to appear. The police promptly issued a 'Wanted' notice, along with a description of Hutchinson – the notice stated he was wanted for murder, by poisoning.

The story quickly became a sensation, and the whole country was caught up in the manhunt. Hutchinson was reported to have fled to London, where it was expected that he would try to leave the country. He was thought to have around £25 on him, was carrying a dark-brown bag, and may have been wearing a dark-coloured coat. In London, he evaded capture a number of times – surprisingly, given that he cut a fairly distinctive figure. He was described as having a peculiar gait – a springy walk, swinging his arms from the elbows. He also dressed unusually, in a coloured suit, winged white collar, bowler hat, and gold rings, a watch and a chain.

The notice was circulated throughout London, in hotels and shipping offices, and soon proved fruitful. He was reportedly spotted at the Strand, and a hotel owner was able to confirm that he had stayed there on the night of Wednesday 15 February. Detective Inspector Laing travelled down to London to work with Scotland Yard, and between the two forces, they established that Hutchinson had acquired two new identities while in London. This enabled Scotland Yard to circulate and updated the 'Wanted' notice.

Hutchinson was eventually apprehended by chance, while staying in a hotel in Guernsey. Despite having ample chance to get a ship to any destination before police realised his where-abouts, he had settled on the Channel Islands. He probably thought that this was a clever solution, as the Channel Islands were not especially far, so the police may not have been check-ing ships to this destination. However, choosing Guernsey may have been a mistake. On a small island, with very few visitors, he stood out far too much. This, coupled with the updated 'Wanted' notice circulated in all the national news-papers, meant that he was easy to spot.

The hotel owner happened to read a newspaper article about Hutchinson, and realised, with some alarm, that he was staying in his hotel. He headed to the local police station, where he was shown a photograph of John Hutchinson, and was able to confirm that this was the man residing in his hotel. The police, armed with a warrant, descended on the small boarding-house. Sergeant Burley of Scotland Yard was the first to enter, leaving a constable stationed outside, in case Hutchinson attempted to escape.

Inside, all was calm. The hotel owner was sitting at the front desk reading a newspaper, which coincidentally contained a photograph of his notorious lodger.

Burley found Hutchinson sitting by the window reading a book, with his back to the door, his right hand in his pocket. Burley asked his name, and Hutchinson replied, 'My name is Henderson.' Burley responded that he believed his name to be Hutchinson, to which Hutchinson insisted that his name was 'Henderson, and I can prove it.'

Burley then asked Hutchinson to accompany him from the hotel. Hutchinson rose from his chair, still keeping his right hand in his trouser pocket. Burley, leaping to the natural conclusion that Hutchinson had a weapon concealed in his pocket, carefully accompanied him to the door. At this point, Hutchinson made a break for it, and ran for the stairs, taking them two at a time, Burley and the constable on his heels. He made it to his bedroom, where he withdrew his hand from his pocket, not containing a weapon as expected, but a small vial of liquid, which he quickly raised to his lips. Burley managed to knock the vial from his hand and wrestled the young man to the floor.

After a short struggle, Hutchinson went limp. Burley ran for a doctor, who was there within minutes. He attempted to pump Hutchinson's stomach, but just a few minutes later, he stopped breathing. A strong smell of prussic acid filled the room, so there could be no doubt as to the cause of death. Hutchinson died within ten minutes, a significantly quicker and less painful death than that of his father and Clapperton.

Hutchinson was, perhaps, aware that he could not continue to evade capture indefinitely, and had planned accordingly. He clearly intended to die rather than be captured by the police, and opted for the very rapid death that prussic acid was known to deliver, obtaining it from his uncle's pharmacy in preparation. He was unconscious almost immediately after taking the acid, so it seems as though his suffering was minimal. The amount of prussic acid (or cyanide, as it is more commonly known) required to kill a man is very small, and it was later determined by the police that the vial of liquid he had tried to drink actually contained enough poison to kill sixteen people. Hutchinson clearly wanted to leave no room for error.

Following the death of Hutchinson, his belongings were searched and an investigation was carried out. Did he intend to die all along, or had he hoped to escape? His belongings revealed that he did not have a return ticket, and he was carrying a vast amount of cash. The cyanide may have been a backup plan against capture, or if his money ran out. It seems more likely that John Hutchinson was near emotional collapse. Having gone off the rails and spiralled into debt, he had murdered his father for his money, though it is rumoured his father's life was insured for just £4,000, a mere fraction of Hutchinson's overall debt. Was his devastation at the funeral a clever act to avoid detection, or genuine remorse for what he had done?

Hutchinson was buried in the local cemetery on Guernsey; there was no request from his family for his body to be returned to Dalkeith, and he was said to have no mourners at his graveside.

To this day, his exact motives remain unclear. His mother survived, although her life hung in the balance for a time. Had Hutchinson intended to kill only his father in order to claim the life insurance, or had he intended to kill his mother too, as punishment for their failure to help him with his debts, of which they were well aware? As the other guests had all survived, perhaps Hutchinson had administered a smaller dose to them, hoping this would be viewed as food poisoning, and that his father and the grocer would be considered unlucky. Whatever the precise circumstances, John Hutchinson was clearly a troubled man, and perhaps it was just good fortune that he did not kill all of the guests at that fatal dinner.

THE BODIES IN THE QUARRY

Date: 1911
Place: Winchburgh

THE BODIES IN THE QUARRY

The disused Hopetoun Quarry was a dangerous place, filled
with monsters. At least, that was the story that parents in
Linlithgow told their children, in the hope of keeping them
away from the deep waters that now filled the quarry. It was a
dangerous, desolate place, and the trees that overhung the pool
added an eerie element to it. The pool was enormous, eight
hundred metres long and nearly forty metres wide and was
accessible only by a single road. Local people found little
reason to go there.

It was a bright sunny day in June 1913 when Thomas Duncan walked the quarry with his friend and colleague, James
Thompson. Duncan worked as a ploughman at nearby Riddrie
Mains Farm, not far from Winchburgh in West Lothian,
and was showing a new farm-hand, Thompson, around the
surrounding areas of the farm. Tired from the long walk and
the summer heat, the pair stopped to rest in the shade of the
trees for a few minutes. Looking out over the quarry, Duncan
spotted something floating in the dirty water.

It appeared to be a bundle of some kind, although, being
covered in algae and twigs, it was hard to identify, and seemed
almost scarecrow-like. It gave the men a sense of unease, as
there was something strange and almost human about it.

They found a broken tree branch and used it to pull the
bundle closer to shore. As it approached, they realised that
they were looking at the bodies of two dead children, tied
together with rope. Horrified, they tried to pull the bodies

ashore, but the rope holding them together broke, and
one floated free. Hurriedly the men went to summon the
police.

When the bodies were pulled from the water, it was immediately clear to the local police that they were looking at a
double murder, the rope tying them together removing all
doubt that this could have been an accidental death. But
who were they? The bodies had clearly been in the water
for a considerable time, as they were bloated and covered in
algae. The local medical examiner, Dr Cross, initially stated
that a post-mortem would be pointless, as the bodies had
deteriorated too far for an examination to yield any results.
Fortunately, the Procurator Fiscal disagreed and ordered the
remains to be taken to the mortuary at Linlithgow.

There, Professor Harvey Littlejohn and Dr Sidney Smith
undertook an examination, and found that a great deal of
information could be discovered from the bodies. The freezing
cold water of the quarry had actually preserved the corpses
extremely well, and the internal organs had suffered no decom-
position at all. The scientists were quickly able to determine that
the corpses were both young boys, aged approximately four and
six years old, and that they were brothers.

The condition of the bodies was so well preserved that
the stomach and its contents remained intact. The boys' last
meal was confirmed as Scotch broth, and the undigested
condition of the food confirmed that they had eaten this only
an hour or so prior to their death. This provided vital clues
for the police as to the location of the murders themselves –
for there to be such a short time between consuming a meal,
and ending up in the quarry, the boys would have to have lived
only a short distance away, and not have been transported
far to be disposed of in its murky waters. Both boys were
dressed identically in poor-quality garments. These had begun
to rot away in the water, but a crucial clue was discovered –

a small faded marking on one of the boys' shirts was visible. This was identified as a stamp from one of the city's poorhouses. The police now had a great deal more evidence to go on.

The actual method of murder could not be determined. The police and pathologists suspected that the boys had walked willingly along the quarry path, most likely being with someone they knew and trusted. This prompted a massive search across Winchburgh and Broxburn, with police officers going from cottage to cottage to enquire about two boys, who would have been missing since before Christmas of 1911. There had been no reports of missing children filed, but some people reported their suspicions about the whereabouts of two young boys, the sons of Patrick Higgins.

Higgins was employed as a labourer at the brickworks. A big man about forty years old, he was an ex-soldier who had seen active service in India. Since returning, he had visited his doctor, claiming he was becoming forgetful and suffering from frequent headaches. The doctor was sympathetic, but could offer no diagnosis for his ailments and was able to do little to help. Higgins was effectively told to grin and bear it. He and his wife coped, despite having little money. Their two boys, John and William, had a roof over their heads and regular meals.

In 1910, disaster struck for Patrick Higgins, when his wife died. After her death, with no extended family for support, Patrick Higgins became the sole carer of his boys. There were two opposing views of Higgins's life at this point. The kinder view suggests that, with the welfare state still unheard of, and with no means of support, Higgins had no choice but to struggle on. The less sympathetic view was that Higgins was already a heavy drinker, and neglectful of his family. The death of his wife merely resulted in two hungry children who were a significant drain on his drinking money.

Locals often saw the two boys with their father, looking neglected, hungry and miserable. At some point in January 1911, someone reported their father to the police, and Higgins was charged with child neglect. John and William were taken into the Dysart poorhouse, which was maintained by the church. The church requested maintenance from Higgins for their upkeep, which Higgins refused to pay. As penance, he was sentenced to two months in prison.

When he was released, the poorhouse released the boys back into Higgins's care – a questionable decision, as they had only recently been taken from him due to neglect. Unwilling or unable to look after his children, Higgins boarded them in the home of a local widow, Elizabeth Hynes, who lived in Brox-burn. Hynes had known Higgins since he was a child, and was happy to house his children as long as Higgins covered the maintenance costs. Higgins, despite working, paid almost nothing to the widow, who could no longer afford to look after the children, and returned them to their father.

The local Inspector of Poor warned Higgins he would be returned to prison if he did not begin to support his children properly, so Higgins had no choice but to care for the boys himself. As a labourer by trade, Higgins often travelled around the Linlithgow area searching for work, and he was obliged to take the boys with him. The wages of a labourer were poor, and were barely enough to feed the three of them, never mind providing a decent home. The three were regularly forced to sleep rough – often in the brickworks, eating meals of stolen potatoes cooked in a campfire.

Sometimes the local people would take pity on the boys. They were so quiet they would often go unnoticed, trailing forlornly after their drunken father. One rainy night in November, a kind woman took them in and gave them a hot meal of Scotch broth. The bedraggled three were later seen trailing the streets – locals paid little attention, as they were used to seeing the threesome roaming in search of shelter. This time, however, Higgins knew exactly where he was going.

He told some conflicting stories to those who encountered him. Hugh Shields, a miner and drinking acquaintance of Higgins, saw him and his sons heading east earlier that evening. Several hours later, Higgins appeared in a local tavern, and spotting Shields, joined him for a drink. Shields questioned Higgins as to the whereabouts of his boys, to which Higgins replied, 'They're all right – they're on their way to Canada now.' What Shields made of this is unknown.

Perhaps if Higgins had stuck to just one story, he might have evaded suspicion. However, another acquaintance had also seen Higgins and the boys that same night. James Daly, another miner, had seen Higgins and the boys walking towards Winchburgh earlier that evening. Several hours later, Higgins appeared in another tavern, soaked to the skin. Daly also enquired as to the whereabouts of the boys, and was given a totally different – and somewhat bizarre – story of the boys' whereabouts. Higgins gave an account of a train journey to Edinburgh, which he had allegedly undertaken with the boys. He claimed they had all boarded the 20:30 train to Edinburgh, where they shared a compartment with a well-to-do lady who had taken a shine to one of the boys, and offered to give him a home.

Higgins claimed his response to this unlikely suggestion was to state that where one boy went, the other must go too. The first lady refused, but another lady in the compartment spoke up and offered to house the other boy. This settled, Higgins bade farewell to his sons, jumped off the train at Ratho, and raced back to Winchburgh for a celebratory drink. Daly, understandably suspicious of this unlikely account, asked if Higgins had taken the addresses of the two ladies. Higgins said not, but that they had taken his. Daly then pointed out that Higgins was effectively homeless and had no such address to give. Higgins triumphantly stated he had given his work address – Winchburgh Brickworks!

Shortly after, Higgins stumbled drunkenly back to the brickworks, where he was currently sleeping. He came across Alexander Fairnie, a brick turner, and told him the story of the ladies on the train, before passing out. Some months later, Fairnie asked him how the boys were getting on in their new homes. Higgins responded unceremoniously that they were both dead. Shortly after, he called in on Mrs Hynes, the kindly widow, and told her that both the boys had drowned. Apparently nobody suspected anything especially untoward at the time, but the later police enquiries, coupled with the description of the boys and Higgins's odd accounts of their disappearance, brought suspicion to the minds of the local people, and quickly directed police to Patrick Higgins.

After a short search, the police discovered Higgins staying at a boarding house in Broxburn. Anticipating resistance, they opted to take him by surprise, and arrived to arrest him at 2 a.m. The innkeeper took them to a bedroom with two occupants. Upon seeing the police, Higgins stood up and confirmed to his room-mate that he believed the police were after him, and left quietly with them.

He was charged with the murder of his sons, and imprisoned pending trial.

His trial started on September 11 1913. In the courtroom, observers reported that he behaved like a soldier, standing to attention when he was addressed by name, and exhibiting no feelings or expression. He pleaded 'Not Guilty' to the murders. The basis of his defence was that there was no evidence to directly tie him to the murders. His defence team also requested a special defence plea to be lodged, stating that he was insane and not responsible for his actions at the time he was alleged to have committed the murders. Higgins appeared to be trying to cover all bases in order to get away with murder.

During the trial, there were reports that Higgins suffered with epilepsy, which had been the reason for his discharge from the army and subsequent return from India. There was a question as to when the epilepsy began. Higgins had served six or seven terms with the Scottish Rifles in India, which would not have been possible if he had been afflicted with epilepsy as a younger man. This raised a question whether there had been any form of brain injury, and whether this could have caused murderous behaviour.

A general practitioner from Kelso gave evidence, stating that Higgins's mother had contacted him shortly after his discharge from the army to check on her son's mental state. She had awoken at some point during the night to find her son in her room, waving a poker around in an agitated fashion. A number of witnesses attested to witnessing Higgins's 'shaking fits', often accompanied by foaming at the mouth, and a full examination by a doctor revealed marks on his head which could have been sustained during an epileptic fit.

Higgins himself had not sought any medical advice for epilepsy and took no medication. He claimed he had been free from epilepsy since India, unless drinking. Several doctors, who all commented on his cold indifference, examined Higgins, but none could find evidence to support an insanity plea. The judge, Lord Johnston, remarked during the trial that 'callousness, cold-bloodedness and deliberate cruelty were not insanity'.

Another factor counting against Higgins was the element of premeditation. If he were not intending to murder his children, why had he been seen by two witnesses leading them in the direction of the quarry? Additionally, when questioned, why had he produced two different accounts of the events? These two points proved damning.

The jury provided a unanimous verdict of 'Guilty', but felt some sympathy towards Higgins, and asked the judge to consider mercy based on the inconclusive medical evidence as to his state of mind at the time of the murders.

The judge sympathised to a degree, but still felt compelled to deliver the death penalty. As Higgins stood to attention, the judge sentenced him to death, but did not don the customary black cap when delivering his verdict, perhaps a symbolic message about the unhappiness of the events and the fate of Higgins.

During his summing up, the judge condemned the church workers at the Dysart poorhouse for returning the boys to the care of their father, despite him having been imprisoned for neglect. The boys had been failed by those charged to care for them. Had those officials done their jobs there might have been a very different outcome.

When the story of the boys' murders first appeared in the press, the initial response was horror and disgust. However, over time some began to see the boys and their killer as victims. The boys were victims of the system, forced into the hands of a man unable to provide the appropriate care, and their helpless and penniless father driven to this desperate act, having no means of support and only the prospect of further jail time if he could not provide for his sons.

A larger than average crowd drew outside Edinburgh's Calton jail on 1 October 1913, the day of the execution. The mood was sombre, lacking the usual celebrations and frivolity. Many lit bonfires and held prayer vigils. When the black flag lifted to signify that Higgins was dead, there was no cheering – instead there were prayers.

Canon Stuart of St Mary's Cathedral revealed afterwards that he had prayed with Higgins, a lapsed Catholic, until his death. The Canon let it be known that Higgins had shared with him his views on the justice of his sentence, and had said,

'Drink, and through drink, neglect of religion has let me down.' Lacking were words relating directly to his boys, but the execution of Patrick Higgins may well have triggered the beginning of a shift in public mood towards showing more care for the more vulnerable members of society. It may be that the death of Patrick Higgins had another purpose, not just punishment.

THE UNGRATEFUL SON

Date: 1926
Place: Edinburgh

It was at the age of sixteen, when he was sent to Malvern College on his arrival from New Zealand, that Donald Merrett's behaviour started to cause his mother concern.

Born John Donald Merrett in New Zealand in 1908, Donald, or Donnie as he was often known, was the only child of Bertha Milner and John Alfred Merrett, an electrical engineer. His parents had met on a voyage to Egypt; his father was en route to New Zealand, where they married. After Donald's birth, John Merrett's work took the family to St Petersburg, but the climate was unsuitable for a small child, so Bertha Merrett left her husband to continue his work, taking young Donald to Switzerland. Then came the outbreak of the First World War, and Donald's father disappeared, believed killed in the Russian Revolution. When the war was over, they returned to New Zealand, and Bertha Merrett assumed sole responsibility for her son's welfare and education.

So it was, in 1924, that Donald took up a place at Malvern College, his mother intent on him pursuing a career in the diplomatic service. His tutors found his work to be excellent, but his conduct less so. He looked mature for his age, already having developed an eye for the ladies, and the habit of spending beyond his means. A little concerned at what her son might get up to at Oxford, Bertha Merrett decided to take a safer option, and arranged for him to attend Edinburgh University; she would rent a flat in the city, and Donald could lodge with

her, enabling her to keep a close watch on both his attendance
and his expenditure.

After living in boarding houses for a short time, Mrs Merrett
found suitable accommodation at 31 Buckingham Terrace, a
substantial house that had been divided into flats. Their flat
consisted of a sitting-room, two bedrooms, a kitchen and a
bathroom. To assist with the upkeep of the flat, Mrs Merrett
secured the services of a maid, Henrietta Sutherland, who
would come in between 9 a.m. and noon each day. They took
over occupation of the flat on 10 March 1926.

Mrs Merrett was a cultured, intelligent woman, well accust-
omed to managing her own affairs. Although her son would
inherit a considerable sum from his grandfather on reaching
the age of twenty-one, she had to manage on about £700
per year, but she managed her finances carefully, enabling
her to pay for her son's education and their joint upkeep.
She was devoted to her son, and she was pleased by the way
he had settled down to his studies since arriving in Edinburgh. He seemed content with the allowance of ten shillings
per week that he received from his mother, retired to bed
at a respectable time each night, and attended his classes
diligently.

The reality of Donald Merrett's life could not have been
more different. After saying good night to his mother, he
would slip away into the night; in their new flat, this was
achieved by means of a rope from the balcony outside his
bedroom. He had discontinued his studies completely, spending his time on racier pursuits. His favourite haunt was the
Dunedin Palais de Danse, a dance-hall where he lavished
presents on a Miss Betty Christie, one of the dance instruc-
tors, whose training services he would hire for thirty shillings
a night, and fifteen shillings for an afternoon. He bought her
jewellery, and transported her around Edinburgh on the back
of his motor bike, which he bought in early March without his

mother's knowledge. For a young man with an income of ten shillings a week, he was living a very high life.

* * *

When the Merrett's maid, Henrietta Sutherland, arrived for work at 9.00 a.m. Wednesday 17 March, she found a normal domestic scene. Mrs Merrett and her son had finished their breakfast in the sitting room, so Henrietta busied herself tidying up the plates. Mrs Merrett had taken writing materials from the bureau, and had settled herself down at the table in the sitting room to write a letter, while her son sat reading in an armchair. With both of them in residence in the small sitting room, the maid decided to leave attending to the fire in there until later, and after going to the cellar to collect some coal, knelt down by the kitchen fire. She had barely begun working on the fire, when the sound of a gunshot echoed around the flat. She rose but remained rooted to the spot, until she heard books falling in the lobby, and Donald Merrett rushed into the kitchen. According to the maid's later testimony, Merrett was distraught, and told her that his mother had shot herself. She replied that Mrs Merrett had seemed quite all right when she had spoken to her, but Merrett replied 'that he had been wasting his mother's money, and he thought she was worried over that'.

On entering the dining room, the maid found Mrs Merrett lying unconscious on her back, between the bureau and the table, with the chair on which she had been sitting overturned. She was bleeding heavily from a head wound, but was still breathing. Glancing around, the maid saw a pistol on the top of the bureau.

Electing to leave Mrs Merrett where she had fallen, they telephoned the police, and waited downstairs at the street door until two constables arrived, together with an ambulance. The forces of law and order did not distinguish themselves on their arrival at the scene; one of the constables picked up the blood-stained pistol, wrapped it up in paper, and put it in his pocket, but afterwards could not recall if he took it from the top of the bureau or from the floor next to Mrs Merrett. His colleague said later that he had seen him pick it up from the floor. Merrett said later that he himself had picked up the pistol, and placed it on the bureau before going into the kitchen.

Having seen his mother safely delivered to the infirmary, Merrett decided to call in to his favourite dance hall, and booked Miss Christie for the day, taking her out on his motor cycle. He told her, and a friend later, that he had been sitting in his armchair reading a book when the gun had gone off, and that he had gone through to the kitchen to tell the maid.

Curiously, that afternoon the maid's account of the story had changed. When Detective-Inspector Fleming and a colleague called at the flat, she told them that, on hearing the shot, she had gone into the lobby in time to see, through the open sitting room door, Mrs Merrett fall from her chair, and the pistol fall from her hand. The detectives noticed on the open bureau that there were two letters from the Clydesdale Bank, addressed to Mrs Merrett, advising her that her account was overdrawn. They noticed also an unfinished letter on the table, but noted no bloodstains upon it.

With attempted suicide clearly confirmed by the maid's account, the detectives returned to the station and recorded the fact accordingly. Suicide being an offence in law, the infirmary were instructed to advise the police when Mrs Merrett was fit enough to be discharged, in order that she be taken into custody. The disparity between the maid's two accounts of what happened was noted, and some days later, a third statement was taken from her, in which she returned to her original story of having remained in the kitchen, dismissing her earlier statement because 'she was excited at the time'. From the point of view of the police, the case was already closed.

Back at the infirmary, Mrs Merrett had been examined, and it had been established that there was a wound from a pistol-shot in her right ear, and that a small bullet was embedded at the base of her skull, but could not be operated on. Despite her injury, Mrs Merrett recovered consciousness on the night of the shooting. She had been placed in a secure ward used for attempted suicides, where the official policy was not to discuss the details of the circumstances surrounding the patient's admission. As a result, when Mrs Merrett came to and com-plained of a pain in her ear, she was told by the doctor attending that she had had 'a little accident'. The following day she had further conversations with the medical staff, recalling that she had been writing a letter when suddenly a bang had gone off in her head like a pistol. In a later con-versation with the doctor attending, she recalled that her son had been standing beside her, waiting to take her letter to post, and that she had told him to go away. Then there was an explosion, and she could recall no more.

The doctor was sufficiently concerned by this to call In-spector Fleming, and tell him of the conversation. However, it was not enough to change the official view of the case, and although Mrs Merrett remained lucid for the next six days, no attempt was made by the police to record an official statement.

The conspiracy of silence within the infirmary was mirrored by the suppression of information outside. Donald Merrett advised medical staff that his mother was on bad terms with her family, and as a result her two sisters were not notified that she had been seriously injured, neither were her friends in Edin-burgh. Merrett's visits were rare, and he gave his contact details as the 'Dunedin Palais'. Eventually, word was passed to a friend, Mrs Hill, who in turn telegraphed one of the sisters,

Mrs Penn, who was away on holiday, and who hurriedly came to Edinburgh with her husband. Both ladies were requested by the medical staff to maintain the story that Mrs Merrett's condition was as a result of a fall, and when she told her sister of how the explosion had gone off in her head 'as if Donald had shot me', Mrs Penn had told her it was impossible.

On the evening of 25 March, Mable Merrett became delirious, eventually lapsing into unconsciousness, and she died on 1 April. Her death was certified as being due to basal meningitis following a bullet wound. The post-mortem, by Professor Littlejohn, concluded that it was not possible to estimate the range from which the shot was fired, but that the position of the wound was consistent with suicide, although the possibility of an accident he felt 'cannot be wholly excluded'.

After the funeral, Mr and Mrs Penn volunteered to look after Donald, and stayed in the flat with him for two months, during which he continued his late-night excursions to the Palais. Merrett had admitted buying the gun 'to shoot rabbits' and in one version of his story, stated that his mother had taken the gun from him, and had put it, still loaded, in the bureau. Mrs Penn clung to the hope that her sister may inadvertently have removed the pistol with a sheaf of papers from the bureau drawer, and that the gun had gone off accidentally. In any event, the notice of her death placed by her relatives in *The Scotsman* stated it to have been 'by accident'.

When the Penns left, responsibility for Donald Merrett's welfare passed to the Public Trustee, and he was despatched to a vicarage in Buckinghamshire to prepare him for his continuing university career.

Part of the duties of the Public Trustee was to establish the late Mrs Merrett's assets, and, as a result, they began to scrutinise her financial records. These showed her to have been meticulous in her book-keeping, but that in the eight weeks leading up to her death, there had been a dramatic change in her spending habits, with over £360 having been drawn out – equivalent to over half of her annual income. On closer inspection, it transpired that the cheques involved were made payable to J. D. Merrett, and had been endorsed and cashed by him, the last two having been issued after his mother had lapsed into unconsciousness for the last time.

On being advised of these findings, the police realised that perhaps their assumption of suicide had been a little hasty. A warrant for Merrett's arrest was issued on 29 November; he was apprehended and taken into custody, and the trial scheduled for 1 February 1927.

* * *

Merrett was to face two charges; the murder of his mother, and the forging of her signature on 29 cheques for a total value of £457.13s.6d. His prosecution by the Crown was the responsibility of the Lord Advocate, the Right Honourable William Watson, K.C., his defence team was headed by Craigie Aitchison, K.C., and Macgregor Mitchell, K.C., with Lord Alness presiding.

The prosecution case progressed predictably; the maid, Henrietta Sutherland, was called, and adhered to her original account, of having remained in the kitchen until Merrett came to find her. Various witnesses confirmed Merrett's purchases – the pistol and ammunition, the second-hand motor cycle and the new racing motor cycle and sidecar for £139 that he had ordered on hire purchase, while his mother lay dying in hospital.

The doctors and nurses who had examined and dressed Mrs Merrett's wound stated that they had seen no blackening of the wound that they would have expected from a pistol discharged at a range consistent with a case of suicide. The medical staff also confirmed that up to the night of 25 March, they considered Mrs Merrett to have been in complete possession of her mental faculties. The defence objected strongly to statements attributed to Mrs Merrett, pointing out that nobody, including the police, had taken down a written record of her words.

It was the medical aspects of the case that became the most hotly debated. Professor Littlejohn, who carried out the postmortem, was obliged to carry out a rather inelegant u-turn, and state that his original assertion that the wound was 'consistent with suicide' was wrong. After further experiments carried out jointly with Professor Glaister of Glasgow, and discussions with the medical staff who attended Mrs Merrett, he concluded that the evidence 'all pointed to the weapon having been fired by another party'. He concluded further that the nature of the wound was such that he had no reason to believe that it would have affected the victim's mental faculties. Professor Glaister took the stand to confirm the conclusion that the wound was inconsistent with suicide.

The defence team had a real heavyweight in their corner. Sir Bernard Spilsbury is frequently described as 'the father of forensic science', his early fame coming from his involvement in the case of Dr Crippen, followed by a steady stream of high-profile murder cases. Sir Bernard's conclusions were diametrically opposed to the Crown's expert witnesses. Having carried out his own experiments with a London gun-maker, he outlined the circumstances in which, by the bleeding from the wound and its cleaning, the tell-tale black deposit, indicating the discharge of the pistol at close range, could easily have been removed without being noticed. He considered that nothing in the nature of the wound precluded suicide.

Another expert witness for the defence, Dr George Robertson, cautioned the wisdom of accepting the statements made by Mrs Merrett, as he could point to similar cases where the wounded party's recollection of events was incomplete or totally erroneous.

If there were elements of doubt regarding the shooting, the matter of the cheque forgery was rather more straightforward. Handwriting and forgery experts outlined the method used, and one of the cheque books used for the forged cheques was found in the basement of the Dunedin Palais. The defence could make no headway in trying to establish an alternative interpretation of the facts.

In summing up for the prosecution, the Lord Advocate pointed out the irrefutable evidence on the charge of forgery, and how that provided the motive for the murder. The overdraft on the account would have betrayed Merrett's activities in the very near future – taking the gun, he shot his mother in the head, with the absence of blackening around the wound confirming it was not a contact wound. The defence case that her death was suicide depended entirely on Mrs Merrett having knowledge of the pistol, and the only verification of the fact was from Merrett himself, and his testimony on this point was inconsistent. Even assuming she knew of the pistol, why would she be sitting calmly writing a letter, and then decide suddenly to shoot herself in front of her son. The Lord Advocate asked that Merrett be found guilty on both counts.

Craigie Aitchison, K.C., rose to his feet to make the closing speech for the defence. He concentrated on the presumption of innocence. Here was a case, he said, brought to court some ten months after the event, with the evidence of Mrs Merrett's statements being recounted by friends and relatives. The police had not considered it necessary to take a formal statement from her, and expert medical evidence had cast doubt on how reliable her statements would have been. He reminded the jury that the Crown's principal witness on the medical evidence had changed his theory completely since the outset of the case, and the only witness present at the scene, apart from Merrett, had, at one stage, testified to police officers that she had seen Mrs Merrett fall to the floor with the pistol in her hand.

Mr Aitchison closed with the following appeal to the jury: 'I claim from you with a clear conscience a verdict of "Not Guilty" upon both these charges. Give him by your verdict a reputation up to which he will have to live for the rest of his life; and I will only say this to you – and it is my final word – send him out from this court-room this afternoon a free man with a clean bill, and, so far as I can judge, he will never dishonour your verdict.'

The Lord Justice Clerk summed up the case for the jury in clear, impartial statements. The accused could only be found guilty of murder if the Crown had excluded suicide or accident as a reasonable hypothesis. He was critical of the police for their lapses throughout the case, from not adequately recording the crime scene, to their notable failure to take any formal statement from Mrs Merrett during the extended period she was able to talk lucidly, leaving the case resting on the recollections of others. Indeed, was the police prosecution solely as a result of the investigation of the forged cheques, there being no evidence to associate the accused with a murder charge otherwise?

The jury took less than an hour to reach their verdict. Later it was revealed that no one had voted for a 'Not Guilty' verdict on the murder; five had voted for 'Guilty', but the remaining ten had voted for that peculiarly Scottish verdict – 'Not Proven'. The verdict on the cheque forgery charge was a unanimous 'Guilty'. Donald Merrett served a one-year sentence in a new model prison at Saughton before walking free.

* * *

Mr Aitchison's hopes for his client's future conduct were soon disappointed. On his release from prison Merrett was offered accommodation in Bexhill by a friend of his late mother, Mrs Bonner. She had a spare room, but she also had a seventeen-year-old daughter called Vera. Within two years of his mother's death, Donald Merrett and Vera had eloped, and married in Glasgow, but within months they had been arrested (giving false names) for obtaining goods by false pretences.

Now calling himself Ronald Chesney, Merrett's trail of deceit continued, leading him to spend six months in Durham jail just before reaching his 21st birthday. It was upon this event that he inherited £50,000 from his grandfather's estate, but soon the money was frittered away, and the years leading up to the Second World War found Merrett becoming involved in blackmail and smuggling. He spent the war years in the Royal Navy Volunteer Reserve, and after the war, leaving his wife living with her mother in Ealing, he set off for the continent, where he became involved in the black market in post-war Germany. Another jail sentence followed for smuggling, and the early 1950s found him with a new girl friend, but short of cash and beginning to ponder on the £8,000 trust fund that he had set up with his wife before he went abroad, the sum being payable to whichever of the two outlived the other.

It was at this stage that Merrett came up with the plan to get his hands on the money. Travelling to England under a false passport, he would murder his wife, making it look like an accident, before slipping back to Germany unnoticed. In February 1954 he put his plan into action. Arriving in England, he made his way to Ealing, where he was reunited with his wife, and after plying her with drink, drowned her in the bath. However, his plan went badly awry as he made to leave the house and was surprised by his seventy-two-year-old mother-in-law. Desperate to conceal his presence in the country, he lashed out at her with a pewter tankard, rendering her unconscious, before strangling her with her own stockings. Concealing her body, he slipped away and out of the country, returning to his home in Cologne, still hopeful that he had escaped detection.

His hope was short-lived. Vera's body was found the day after her murder, and her mother's body found in the subsequent search. The murder hunt that followed established that Ronald Chesney was Donald Merrett, and a full-scale search was soon under way. As Merrett read news of the pursuit, it was clear to him that he would be unable to evade justice this time. On 16 February 1954, six days after the double murder, he walked into a wood outside Cologne, put the barrel of his Colt revolver in his mouth, and pulled the trigger.

His funeral in Cologne was attended by four people: an official from the British government, a photographer, his German girlfriend and another woman who was found to have married him some years previously. To the list of his crimes had been added that of bigamy.

THE POLISH SOLDIER

Date: 1947
Place: Perthshire

The invasion of Poland by Germany in September 1939 marked the beginning of the Second World War. Poland never formally surrendered, but within five weeks the occupation of Poland by German and Russian forces was complete. The remnants of the Polish armed forces joined the allies in their fight to try and stop the inexorable march of Nazi forces across Europe. When France fell in 1940, a contingent of the Polish army was sent to Scotland for re-training in the use of British equipment. In the struggle towards ultimate victory over the next five years, Polish forces on land, on the sea and in the air made a significant contribution.

When the war ended in 1945, Poland was under the rule of a Communist regime, and many exiled Poles chose not to return to the land of their birth. At this time there were 200,000 Polish soldiers stationed in Britain, and the Polish Resettlement Act 1947 offered British citizenship to those who wished to stay. Various resettlement centres were set up, providing accommodation and food for the ex-soldiers while they found themselves jobs and began their gradual integration into British society.

Taymouth Castle was one such resettlement centre, and it gave valuable support to around eight hundred Polish soldiers who had decided to remain in Scotland. The castle had a commanding view over the surrounding countryside, and one of the sights that could hardly fail to be noticed was Tower Cottage, on Bolfracks Hill above Loch Tay. The cottage was eye-catching in style, as it was significantly different to the traditional style of highland cottage. It was built sturdily from a number of different materials, and in varying designs, but most unusually it had a small watch-tower.

The cottage had attracted the attention of one particular resident of the castle, Stanislaw Myszka. Myszka was a twenty-three-year-old Pole, whose family had been left in France. He was interested in the cottage, and made enquiries about its occupants. It was owned by a married couple called McIntyre; the husband was the head shepherd on the Tombuie estate, and they had three children, a son and two daughters. In a small community such as this, the locals were all aware of the McIntyres' employment circumstances, and the fact that one of Mr McIntyre's duties was to distribute the weekly wages to the other estate staff, which meant that he would have about £90 in cash in his possession at certain times. Myszka had become impatient with life at the resettlement centre, and decided that he could start a new life far more quickly if he could get his hands on a substantial amount of cash. The McIntyres became the obvious target.

In late September, Myszka put his plan into action. Using his military training he set up a concealed hiding-place just a few hundred yards from the McIntyres' cottage. While not the most comfortable of situations, it enabled him to watch his targets for a couple of days, gaining familiarity with the pattern and timing of their movements.

On Friday, 26 September 1947, Myszka was watching the cottage from a safe distance, hidden in the bracken. The McIntyres had a small terrier as a pet, and Myszka was aware that he could not risk getting too close. If the dog detected his presence or scent, it would bark endlessly, which would most likely prompt investigation. He had been there for most of the night, patiently waiting for McIntyre and his son to leave for work. McIntyre's job as head shepherd meant he left for work extremely early in the morning. His son, Archie, was also employed on the estate as a farm worker. He left the house at around 8 a.m., leaving his mother in the house alone. The McIntyres' two daughters, Mary and Annie, were safely away on holiday in the Isle of Arran.

As he left home, Archie paused briefly, spotting a small movement in the bracken, which stood several feet high. He considered investigating, but realised that any movement was likely to have been caused by one of the many deer that roamed the estate, and continued on his way to work. Myszka, concealed in the bracken, had made a mistake and moved slightly. This mistake could well have led to his discovery. It is fortunate for Archie that he chose not to investigate, as Myszka was armed with a sawn-off shotgun, which he would not have hesitated to use.

The forty-seven-year-old Catherine McIntyre was left at home alone for the day. Instead of washing up the breakfast dishes straight after breakfast as usual, she chose to leave them for the moment. She was missing her holidaying daughters a great deal, and decided that she would write them a letter. She was expecting the postman at 10 a.m., and wanted to complete the letter before he arrived. Tower Cottage was set a significant distance from the town and in a relatively isolated location, so it was far easier for the postman to collect the letter when dropping off the normal post than for Catherine to travel to the nearest post-box some distance away. She was not due to leave the house until later that afternoon, when she had made arrangements to visit a friend, Mrs McKerracher, who lived at one of the nearby farms with her husband.

As Catherine McIntyre settled at the table to write her letter, Myszka, satisfied that she was alone and that neither Archie nor Mr McIntyre was likely to return, began to approach the house at some speed. It is not known whether he knocked on the door, or merely broke in. It is likely that the terrier heard his approach and alerted Catherine to his presence. Whether he entered the cottage with murderous intent is also not known. He may have intended to break in merely to steal the cash, and any other valuables he could secure, using the shotgun only to frighten Catherine, or he may have murdered her to ensure she could not report his description to the police.

While it is unknown exactly what happened in those few minutes, Catherine did not survive the break-in. Myszka made his escape and hurried back to his temporary lair. It is suspected that this is where he quickly changed out of his overalls, dry-shaved his face, and dressed in a new – stolen – suit. He deposited the bloodstained overalls, razor, and several other items in the bracken.

At 10 a.m., as usual, the postman knocked on the door. He was surprised to receive no answer but assumed that Mrs McIntyre had gone out, so merely left the newspapers on the doorstep and continued on his way. Nobody else called at the house that day until after 5 p.m., when Archie returned home for his dinner. He found the dog outside, barking loudly, and all the doors locked. His mother was always home when he arrived back from work, so he did not carry a set of keys with him. He knocked a couple of times, puzzled at the lack of response, then remembered Catherine had mentioned at breakfast that she would be out visiting her friend that afternoon. He assumed she had been delayed, and perhaps lost track of time chatting to her friend. Not unduly concerned, and expecting she would arrive shortly, Archie settled on the doorstep with the newspapers while he awaited her return.

A few minutes later, he was startled to see Mrs McKerracher hurrying anxiously towards him. She had been expecting Catherine for tea earlier in the afternoon, first assuming she had been delayed, but gradually becoming more concerned at this out-of-character behaviour, and had come to check that nothing was wrong. Archie told her that the house was locked up, with no response to his repeated knocking. The pair wondered with growing concern whether Catherine had been taken ill, or had somehow injured herself inside the house, and was unable to get to the door.

With no sign of Mr McIntyre, Archie fetched a ladder and used it to break into the house through the kitchen window. A strange sight confronted him. The breakfast plates remained in the sink, and the partially-finished letter to her daughters lay on the table. The letter stopped mid-sentence, which seemed odd to Archie. He called out to his mother, with no response. With growing unease, he searched the lower floor of the house before moving upstairs. He called out to Catherine several times, still with no response. Systematically, he searched all the rooms, before discovering his own bedroom door was locked.

With growing trepidation, Archie knocked, again receiving no answer. At this point, he fetched an axe and broke down the door. He was confronted by his mother's body, lying on one of the beds in his room. Her hands and feet were bound with black bootlaces, and she had been beaten severely around the head. The mattress from the other bed had been placed on top of her body.

The police were called, and a number of officers quickly arrived on the scene. A much-shaken Archie helped them to search the house and determine what had been stolen. One of Archie's suits, Catherine's wedding ring and £90 in cash had all disappeared. Archie recalled the movement he had seen in the bracken that morning, and pointed out the spot to the officers. They discovered a set of bloodstained overalls, a scrap of bloodstained handkerchief, a razor-blade, with a number of very short hairs attached to it, and the shotgun, which had been broken into pieces. There was blood on the butt. It appeared the police had found their murder weapon.

Also at the scene was a train ticket from Perth to Aberfeldy. Police investigated this with the issuing rail station, and it was confirmed that this type of ticket was issued only to soldiers, and that a number of Polish soldiers had travelled on the route the previous day. This directed the investigating officers to Taymouth Castle, where, with the help of an interpreter, they undertook the laborious task of interviewing all eight hundred current residents. With no description of the perpetrator to go on, the police were unable to narrow down the suspect list any further than this. However, the police also issued a description of the murder weapon, and were contacted by an Aberdeen-shire gardener, who thought that the weapon may have been one that he had lent to one of his farm workers. The farm worker had reported back to the gardener that he had discovered the gun missing when he came to use it.

The police interviewed the farm worker, who advised them during questioning that a Pole by the name of Stanislaw Myszka had previously been employed on the farm, and had since moved south to Perth during the week of the murder. The farmer and his wife were also able positively to identify the scrap of handkerchief as one that they had given to him. With the help of the farmer, police were able to put together an accurate description of Myszka, and the following description was circulated to the general public: 'He is about 35 years of age, 5 ft 6 ins, slim build, thin face, pointed chin and clean-shaven, he suffers from a spasmodic cough which is at times quite severe.' Stanislaw Myszka was now officially wanted for the murder of Catherine McIntyre and the police investigation widened.

The police were contacted by another Polish exile, Wlady-stow Szwec. Szwec was a friend of Myszka and had been visited by him the day after the murder. Szwec reported that Myszka, who had previously been chronically short of money, had come to visit dressed in a smart suit. Szwec's wife had been reading the paper during his visit, and had actually read details of the murder aloud from the newspaper in Myszka's presence. Szwec reported that the Pole's face had 'reddened like a fire' upon hearing the details of the killing.

The net was closing fast. A taxi driver, who may have driven Myszka from Aberfeldy to Perth sometime after the murder, contacted the police. He reported picking up a foreigner, who appeared dishevelled and as though he may have been sleeping rough. The foreigner had paid his fare from a thick roll of banknotes. More evidence mounted when the wife of a fellow-soldier at Taymouth Castle reported seeing Stanislaw Myszka shortly after the murder. He appeared smartly dressed, and had taken the soldier and his wife for a shopping spree. This behaviour was definitely out of character for Myszka, who was perpetually short of money.

The police eventually caught up with Myszka at a former RAF base in Portside, where he had been sleeping in one of the disused huts. After a long chase across the airfield, he was eventually apprehended and was arrested on the spot. When searched, Catherine McIntyre's wedding ring was discovered in his shoe. He was still wearing the suit stolen from Archie McIntyre, which, while smart, was several sizes too big for him and gave him a slightly comical appearance.

Myszka was taken to jail to await trial. A Professor Glaister conducted the post-mortem on Catherine's body, and ruled cause of death as 'fracture of the base of the skull, followed by subdural haemorrhage, a result of considerable violence, together with superimposed respiratory embarrassment'. In simpler terms, Catherine had been beaten about the head, and finally suffocated by the mattress in the bedroom. Professor Glaister had a considerable professional interest in hair, and undertook some analysis of the small hairs found on the discarded razor-blade found in the woods. He requested samples of Myszka's shaving hairs to be brought to him from

Perth Prison, and undertook a comparison of the two samples. Before the discovery of DNA, a definite comparison could not be made, but Professor Glaister was able to determine from microscopic analysis that the two samples were very closely matched in colour, as were their 'gross and detailed structural characteristics'. This evidence was presented at Myszka's trial, with the caveat that this could not be considered a certain match, but that the similarity was strong enough for it to be highly probable that both hair samples came from Myszka.

Myszka tried hard to escape the death penalty, and his lawyer lodged a request for an insanity plea to be lodged. This would always be difficult to achieve in a case such as this, where the motive of the murder was clearly for personal and financial gain and the robbery had been planned days before execution. The plea was carefully considered, as the atrocities and horrors experienced by the Pole throughout the war, coupled with his settling in an unfamiliar land, may have resulted in a disturbed mental state. The request for an insanity plea was ultimately thrown out when it was noted that all eight hundred residents at Taymouth Castle had suffered the same circumstances, and had not murdered anyone. Rumours circulated that Myszka had been 'sick with worry' over his children. It was reported that his children had been living safely in France, but were shortly due to be repatriated to Poland.

Regardless of the circumstances, Myszka had committed cold-blooded murder, and the jury spent little time in reaching a verdict of 'Guilty'.

He was hanged in Perth Prison on 6 February 1948, the last hanging to have taken place there.

THE BEAST OF BIRKENSHAW

Date: 1957
Place: Glasgow

It was in September 1956 that police were called to a house in the small town of Bothwell, outside Glasgow, to investigate a report of a burglary. A Mr and Mrs Platt and their son had returned from holiday, to find that their house had been ransacked, and that tins of food had been opened and the contents thrown around the kitchen and other rooms. Mud on the bed showed where someone had lain there with shoes on, there were strange holes in the mattress and quilt, and cigarette burns in the carpet. A few items were found to be missing, which included an unusual electric shaver made locally by Phillips, which was not yet available for sale to the general public. The police report was filed, but with no clues as to the identity of the culprit, the prospect of detection seemed remote.

Sharp at nine o'clock on the morning of Monday, 17 September, Helen Collinson, a domestic help, arrived as usual at the bungalow of the Watt family in Burnside, Glasgow, and made her way round to the back door, which was always left open for her by Vivienne Watt, the seventeen-year-old daughter, as she left for college. Mrs Collinson was surprised to find the door locked, so made her way to the window of Vivienne's bedroom where, through a small gap in the curtains, she could see Vivienne still in bed. Assuming she had overslept, she knocked on the window, but the girl remained motionless.

Walking round to the front of the bungalow, she noticed that a pane of glass next to the front door had been smashed, and as she stood wondering what to do next, the postman arrived. After a hurried consultation, they agreed they should investigate further, so the postman reached gingerly through the broken pane, and opened the front door. Receiving no response to their calls, Mrs Collinson opened the door to the bedroom of Marion Watt, Vivienne's mother. Marion Watt was an invalid, and her sister, Margaret Brown, often came to stay. In the dimly-lit bedroom, Mrs Collinson could see the sisters in bed, apparently peacefully asleep, the bed clothes pulled up under their chins. It was only the small trickle of blood from their nostrils that betrayed the fact that they had both been shot in the head at close range.

Appalled, the postman ran to the phone to call the police, while Mrs Collinson, with grim foreboding, made for Vivienne's bedroom. Immediately it was apparent that she had suffered the same fate, her pillow soaked in blood. She gave a low moan, but by the time the police and ambulance arrived she too had died.

As the police forensic team began their examination of the crime scene, police officers started calling on the Watts's neighbours. They were soon able to establish that William Watt, Marion Watt's husband, was away on a fishing trip, and that his wife and daughter had been due to join him the following weekend. Watt, a baker and ex-policeman, had been ill recently, so had gone to recuperate with a few days of leisure, and had taken the family's black labrador with him.

While word was sent to William Watt, detectives began to piece together the events of the last few hours in the Watt household. They learned that Deanne Valente, a friend of Vivienne's who lived next door, had been listening to Radio Luxembourg with Vivienne the previous evening. They enjoyed listening to the 'Top Twenty', which started at eleven o'clock, and Deanne had left at eleven-fifty, although she could hear from her bedroom the sound of Vivienne's radio playing the current number one, *Que Sera, Sera* by Doris Day.

It appeared likely that the women had been killed in the early hours of the morning, but none of the neighbours, or the night-watchman on a nearby building site, had heard the shots. Police enquiries then established that there had been a burglary just a few doors down from the Watts' bungalow. The owners were away on holiday, and entry had been made by smashing the glass next to the front door, and reaching through to unlock it. The intruder had stolen some jewellery, but not before he had helped himself to tins of soup and spaghetti, which he had consumed while sitting on the settee, stubbing out cigarettes on the carpet next to him.

The newspapers were soon on the story, and dubbed the murderer 'The Top Twenty Killer'. The police notified them that Vivienne's clothes had been ripped, and some removed, but there was no indication of any sexual interference. This aspect of the case struck a chord, and the day after the murders, the *Evening Times* pointed out the similarity with the murder of a girl called Anne Kneilands earlier in the year. She had gone missing while walking home late on January night, and had been found battered to death on a golf course, her clothes in disarray in a similar fashion to Vivienne's. Investigations had failed to find her killer.

Another factor in the Watt case was the curious incident that had occurred in William Watt's bakery earlier in September. A man had entered the shop, his collar pulled up and his hat low over his eyes, and pulled a gun on the shop-assistant. Not surprisingly, she screamed loudly, and the gunman left hurriedly.

The prospect of a cold-blooded killer prowling the streets, breaking into ordinary people's houses and murdering them in their beds, was a terrifying one, and was fully exploited by the newspapers, as pressure mounted on the police to find the murderer before he struck again. Although they were pursuing a number of lines of enquiry, the police were starting to focus their attention on William Watt. Friends and family had told the police how devoted he was to his invalid wife, but their investigations had revealed that he had been unfaithful more than once. Watt had testified that he had been asleep in his hotel bed on the night of the murder, and had planned to set off at 5.30 the following morning, but had slept through his alarm, and had finally awoken at 7.30. He left the hotel briefly to reconnoitre his fishing spot for the day, before returning for breakfast at 8.30.

A hotel guest in the room next to Watt's testified that he had heard the alarm go off at 5.30 a.m., and that it had rung for a considerable time before it stopped; the police were surprised that this had not been sufficient to awaken Mr Watt – had he been there. A police driver did the journey from the hotel to Watt's home in a little over two hours, more than enough time for Watt to have driven home in the early hours of the morning, murdered his family, and returned to the hotel between 5.30 and 7.30 a.m. The case against him became even more serious when he was identified as having driven his car on to the Renfrew ferry at 3 a.m. on the day of the murder, a big black dog in the car with him. On Thursday 27 September, William Watt was charged with the three murders, and sent to Barlinnie Prison to await trial, where he would spend the next sixty-seven days. Little did the police know that the real killer was already in the same prison.

* * *

William Watt was represented by one of Scotland's finest criminal lawyers, Lawrence Dowdall, and it was Dowdall who received a letter from a man called Peter Manuel, who was in prison for robbing a local colliery. Manuel claimed to have detailed knowledge of the murders, which he verified by giving a detailed description of the interior of the bungalow, and stating that one of the women had been shot twice in the head, a detail known only to the police. Manuel said he had got the information from an informant, who had also told him of another break-in, during which he had accidentally fired his gun, a .38 Webley, into a mattress while arguing with a female accomplice. Dowdall visited Manuel in Barlinnie Prison, where Manuel had continued to maintain that his information came from a third party. Police enquiries established that Manuel himself had purchased a Webley revolver one week before the murders.

Peter Manuel was already well-known to the police. He was born in New York in 1927, his parents Scottish emigrants who had left their native Lanarkshire to escape the poverty of their existence there, but when Manuel was ten his father became ill, and they returned to Scotland, before settling in Coventry. Always an outsider, he was caught after breaking into a shop, thereby beginning a series of incarcerations in borstals and remand homes, from which he would escape with some ease, enjoying the attention and notoriety that his activities brought him. His thefts soon began to involve increasing levels of violence; at the age of fifteen, he broke into a girl's bedroom and hit her around the head with a hammer, before stealing her purse. Further attacks on women, and a long list of house-breaking charges, saw him given a nine-year sentence in Peterhead Prison in Glasgow.

Desperate for attention, Manuel became known as a fantasist among his fellow prisoners, inventing skills he did not possess and exploits that he had never carried out. When this failed to impress, he began to play the role of the 'hard nut', attacking prison guards, and spending a substantial amount of time in solitary confinement as a result. On his release, he attempted to establish himself as part of the Glasgow underworld, but no one would take him seriously. He was fond of his parents, and on his release from jail, he made some attempt to live a more conventional life, but in 1955 he was arrested for assaulting a woman at knife-point, although he did not rape her. At the ensuing trial, Manuel defended himself, and escaped with a 'Not Proven' verdict.

At the time of the murder of Anne Kneilands in 1956, Manuel was working for the gas board, and was one of a number of employees interviewed. The fact that he had scratches on his face attracted the attention of the police, which increased when they saw his history of theft and violence. A search warrant was obtained for his parents' house, where he lived, but nothing was found to link him with the crime, and he was released. However, he continued to pester the police, writing letters tipping them off about crimes he clearly knew nothing about. To his fellow-prisoners, he would claim, adopting an American accent, to have been an associate of Al Capone, and to have been the criminal mastermind behind major bank raids. At one stage he briefly attracted the attention of the U. S. government by claiming to have knowledge of the escape of the Russian spies Burgess and Maclean.

It is not hard to imagine that there must have been a strong element of scepticism as far as the police were concerned regarding Manuel's involvement in the Watt murders, but the detail he had provided obliged them to take it seriously. So it was that the police, armed once again with a search warrant, descended on the house and garden of Manuel's unfortunate parents, and once again found nothing to link him with the crime under investigation.

William Watt was released from prison in December, after his lawyer effectively discredited his client's identification by the ferryman. With the police investigation apparently stalled, Watt decided to begin his own enquiries. Having established that certain pubs in Glasgow were frequented by known criminals, he started to visit them, to pass on the word that he was looking for information on Peter Manuel, and such was the contempt in which Manuel was held in the criminal fraternity that Watt received a considerable amount of support in return over the following months.

Still claiming his version of events to be true, Manuel was released from Barlinnie Prison in November 1957. There was growing conviction among many of the detectives involved in the case, and newspaper editors, that Manuel was the murderer, but with no evidence to support their theory, Manuel remained at large. This would prove to have a high cost in human lives.

* * *

Eight days after his release from jail, Manuel travelled to Newcastle in an unsuccessful bid to find work. Hailing a taxi outside Newcastle station, he asked the driver to take him to Edinburgh. Later, the cab was found damaged on a quiet moorland road in County Durham, and the body of the cabbie, Sydney Dunn, nearby. He had been shot in the back of the head, and his throat cut.

On his return to Glasgow, Manuel and Watt agreed to meet. Manuel continued to maintain that his knowledge came from a petty thief and his girlfriend who were responsible for the murders, after they had burgled the Watts' house by mistake. Watt was increasingly certain that Manuel was the killer, but managed to control his emotions, apart from one occasion when he threatened violence if he discovered that Manuel had murdered his family. 'People don't do that to Peter Manuel,' was the cool reply, at which point he took a picture from his pocket, and tore it up. It was a picture of the murdered girl, Anne Kneilands.

Meanwhile, just before Christmas in 1957, Mr and Mrs Platt, who had suffered the rather strange break-in in September of the previous year, moved house. The process of moving seemed to have dislodged something in their mattress, and on further investigation, they found this to be one of the watches they had thought stolen during the burglary. Further probing unearthed a bullet, which they passed to the police. Ballistics tests established that the spent bullet had come from the .38 revolver used in the killings of the Watt family.

On Christmas Day, a vicar and his wife came home to find that they had been burgled, and were missing a camera, some new gloves and some cash. Three days later, a girl who lived just a short distance from the vicar's house went missing. Isabelle Cooke had set out in the early evening to catch a bus to meet her boyfriend, but had never arrived. Her walk to the bus stop would have taken her down a deserted footpath, and at 7.30 p.m. a scream was heard by a woman in a nearby house, but she did not investigate and heard no further noise. A police search was instigated the following day, discovering her handbag under a railway bridge, but of Isabelle there was no trace.

But further horror was to follow. On 2 January 1958, a car was found abandoned in the Gorbals area of Glasgow. The owner was found to be Peter Smart, who worked for a civil engineering company, but telephone calls to his house failed to elicit a response. On 6 January, when Smart was due to return to work after the Christmas break, he failed to arrive, so a foreman was sent round to his house to check on him. The foreman found milk and newspapers outside the front door, and on getting no reply to his repeated knocking, called the police. When the police entered the house they found newspapers dating back to 31 December by the front door; climbing the stairs, they entered the main bedroom to find Peter Smart and his wife in bed – they had both been shot through the head. In an adjoining bedroom, they found that the couple's eleven-year-old son had suffered the same fate. The investigating officers noted that Mrs Smart's nightdress had been ripped open.

There was little doubt that the family had been dead for some days, but questioning of the neighbours revealed there had been activity in the house during that period. Smart had drawn out £35 in cash from his bank on 31 December in anticipation of going away to visit relatives for the New Year. On New Year's Day, a neighbour noticed the garage doors were open, but that the car had gone. As they were still open the following day, the neighbour closed them, noticing the curtains were drawn in the house. During the day, a passer-by noticed that the curtains were closed, but that the windows were open, and the following night, a light was seen in the dining-room. On the morning of 4 January, the lounge curtains were open, but the windows closed once more. It was apparent that the killer had spent some days going to and from the house, making himself meals, and feeding the family cat. It was discovered later that a police constable had been given a lift in Smart's stolen car on 2 January, the driver discussing with him the search for Isabelle Cooke, which the constable was about to join. As the policeman climbed out, the driver coolly remarked, 'They're searching in the wrong place.'

The newspapers were now full of the exploits of 'The Beast of Birkenshaw'. The details of the crime sickened not just the general public, but the Glasgow underworld too, and the police found themselves receiving a stream of information about Manuel's activities. He had been seen spending new banknotes freely on New Year's Day, and details of the pubs where he had been drinking were provided. On visiting the pubs in question, police officers were able to recover some of the notes; the serial numbers tallied with the sequence of notes issued by the dead man's bank. For the third time, police raided the Manuel family home, and this time their search bore fruit. More of the new banknotes were found, together with the vicar's camera and gloves, and the distinctive electric razor stolen from the Platt's house. Manuel's father was arrested in connection with the break-ins, and Manuel taken in for questioning.

Manuel claimed to have been given the banknotes by a well-known Glasgow criminal, Samuel McKay, so the police brought in McKay, and made Manuel repeat his assertions to McKay's face. Doing so effectively sealed Manuel's fate. McKay made it his business to supply detailed information about Manuel's activities – the guns he had obtained, the boasts he had made regarding the murders, and precise times and dates.

Manuel maintained his reserve until finally, at a meeting with several senior police officers and his parents, his mother asked him to tell the truth, and he did. Admitting to the murders of the Watt and Smart families, and Anne Kneilands, he also led them to where he had buried Isabelle Cooke after strangling her with her bra. On his directions, the two murder weapons were recovered from the Clyde.

On Monday 12 May, Peter Manuel's trial began. Immaculately dressed in a blazer and grey trousers, he pleaded 'Not Guilty' to the charge of eight murders, three counts of house-breaking and one of simple theft, then maintained his silence for the next three days. His defence team maintained that he had alibis for the time of the killing of the Smart family and the two lone women, but there was a sensation when they announced that Manuel accused William Watt of murdering his own family. There was further sensation when, on the fourth day, Manuel dismissed his legal team and proceeded to conduct his own defence. For the next twelve days he bathed in the spotlight of publicity. Stating that his confession had been extracted from him by the police by means of threats, as part of their plan to frame him for the murders, he spun an elaborate tissue of lies. Reiterating his accusations against William Watt, and placing his parents on the stand to support his alibis, he went so far as to assert that he had obtained the gun at Peter Smart's request. Smart, he claimed, had subsequently used it to shoot his wife and his son, before killing himself, Manuel removing the gun from Smart's lifeless hand when he visited the house, and disposing of it to protect himself.

The judge in his summing-up concluded that Manuel had conducted his defence 'with a skill that is quite remarkable', but the jury could hardly have failed to notice how his account of events would change constantly. After sixteen days of the trial, the jury of nine men and six women retired to consider their verdict. They took only two and a half hours to return, pronouncing him guilty of seven counts of murder, there being insufficient evidence, his confession notwithstanding, to convict him of the murder of Anne Kneilands. The murder of the taxi-driver, having taken place in England, was excluded from proceedings.

Donning the black cap the judge, Lord Cameron, pronounced sentence of death by hanging, to take place at Barlinnie Prison on 19 June 1858. When his subsequent appeal was turned down, Manuel attempted suicide by swallowing disinfectant, but failed and was closely guarded thereafter.

At precisely 8.00 a.m. on 19 June, Harry B. Allen entered the condemned cell. With practised precision he led Manuel to the scaffold in the adjoining room. 'Turn up the radio and I'll go quietly,' were Manuel's last words. By 8.01 he was dead. During his last imprisonment, Manuel had confessed to killing three more women, one in London in 1954, two in Glasgow in 1956, but the police believed he was responsible for even more.

In 2008, an interesting postscript to the case came to light. A consultant neurologist was said to have examined Manuel before the trial, and concluded that he had 'temporal lobe epilepsy' which, coupled with his psychopathic tendencies, could explain his behaviour. If the testimony had been heard in court, then he could have been adjudged to be insane. His decision to defend himself meant the evidence was never heard, and effectively condemned him to death.

SHEILA GARVIE

Date: 1968
Place: Kincardineshire

It was in November 1968 that a murder trial took place in Aberdeen, which revealed a sordid tale of sexual deviancy, orgies and murder that created a sensation in the press.

Sheila Watson was considered by many to be one of the brightest and most beautiful women in her small Scottish community. Sheila was brought up in a strict household; her father, a dour and humourless man, was a stonemason working on the royal estates at Balmoral. As soon as she was old enough, Sheila was found employment in the castle as a domestic servant, but the work bored her, and she found herself a job working in an office. This was much more to her liking, and soon she developed an active social life with the women at the office.

At a dance one night, Sheila encountered Max Garvie. Garvie was one of the more eligible bachelors; handsome, debonair and wealthy, he was not short of admirers, but Sheila caught his eye. They had a brief courtship, and married in June 1955, when Sheila was eighteen and Max twenty-one. Garvie was a rich farmer, living at West Cairnbeg in Kincardineshire. Sheila discovered that the marriage was not all that she had hoped it would be; Max had firm ideas about the role his wife should play, and she was regularly called upon to lay on huge spreads of food for their friends and acquaintances.

The Garvies had two daughters, closely followed by a son in 1964. The young family lived in a luxury home in Laurence-kirk, near Angus, and appeared to enjoy a perfect way of life. Still in their late twenties, they seemed to have everything they could desire – a comfortable lifestyle, healthy children and a loving and supportive relationship.

Initially, the couple were very happy; they had plenty of money to treat themselves to luxuries in life. This was the 1960s, the heyday of sex, drugs and rock and roll. Max Garvie was a big fan of all three activities.

Although Max was officially a farmer, he rarely worked, preferring instead to delegate the work to others while he collected the profits; he had plenty of free time for leisure activities. For a time, his fast cars kept him occupied, and when this no longer satisfied his need for excitement, he progressed to his own aeroplane, a German-built Bolkow Junior. He would frequently fly his plane over the North Sea, usually performing daredevil stunts. Often he would be drunk or high on tranquillisers at the time – and not infrequently both. Max was a heavy drinker, usually going through at least five bottles of whisky in a week. He would mix this with handfuls of Pro-Plus, a caffeine-based stimulant, to keep himself awake, but was dependent on Soneryl, a popular but highly addictive sleeping tablet on the market at the time, to make himself sleep.

Over time, Max's drink and drug habit became heavier, and his leisure activities became more extreme. Sheila began to suffer from bouts of depression; her husband's moods were volatile and unpredictable, and more than once he was violent towards her, on one occasion threatening to shoot her. His sexual appetites were voracious, but Sheila found him increasingly disgusting and perverted. Bored with their sex life, Max branched into erotic photography and naturism, in which he tried to involve his wife and young daughters.

Garvie arranged for a barrier of bushes and trees to be planted on the boundary of his property. The trees formed a triangle, which outsiders assumed was to help protect the farmland from the strong north-easterly winds, and thought little of it. In fact, the trees actually formed a suitable cover for the nudist colony he had set up in his back garden. These times were not for the self-conscious and Garvie set about inviting his friends over to his new colony. It proved popular with Max's well-to-do friends, who found the whole pastime daring and risqué.

After a while, Max was no longer satisfied with just nudity, and began to crave a new thrill. This was when the sex orgies started. They started off relatively low-key, with Max inviting only close friends. Sheila was not keen and refused to participate; she wanted a more straightforward lifestyle which would allow her to spend time with her children. Her vision of the good life definitely did not involve group sex. Garvie began to see Sheila as boring and unadventurous, and their relationship began to sour. Max would taunt Sheila, calling her old-fashioned and a square. He was persuasive and would cajole her, asking her how she knew she would not like it if she never even tried. Eventually Max wore Sheila down and she gave in.

The Garvies' lifestyle was extravagant, and they were not shy about displaying their wealth. Max updated his cars constantly, and continued to fly his private plane on a regular basis. Sheila was always dressed in the most exclusive fashions available, all of which flaunted her enviable figure and left little to the imagination. Despite Max Garvie inviting only close friends to their sex sessions, they were not particularly discreet; the local people began to suspect what was going on, and gossip spread.

The sexual revolution might have been sweeping through Britain, but it had not swept as far as the north-east coast of Scotland. The villagers in this well-off community were straight-laced Doric-speaking people, and disapproved of the activities the Garvies indulged in behind closed doors. They nicknamed the Garvies' home 'Kinky Cottage'.

If the locals disapproved of the Garvies, for Sheila life in 'Kinky Cottage' was not rosy either. Max was becoming more

and more extreme, and continued to seek new highs. His drink
and drug ingestion increased, the orgies continued; he regularly engaged in sex with other women and occasionally men,
by way of variety, but nothing satisfied him for long.

He stumbled on his next project while doing some work for
the Scottish National Party. He got to know a young man by
the name of Brian Tevendale, who was twenty at the time. It is
highly likely that Garvie himself was attracted to Tevendale,
and he took to inviting Tevendale home for dinner with
himself and Sheila. His idea was that Tevendale could take
care of Sheila for him, as he had designs on Tevendale's sister,
Trudy, who was married to a policeman. He would leave
Tevendale alone with Sheila on a regular basis, and when he
returned later, he would interrogate Sheila, demanding to
know if she had had sex with Tevendale. Sheila insisted she
had not. Despite her husband encouraging it, she considered
it a betrayal to have sex with another man without her husband being there.

Garvie hounded her constantly to sleep with Tevendale, and
eventually she did. Brian Tevendale was woken in the night to
find Sheila being unceremoniously shoved into his bedroom
by Garvie, who then shut the door and disappeared. Sheila had
finally given in to her husband's unusual demands. Tevendale
was more than happy to go along with this arrangement;
despite being eleven years his senior, Sheila was still extremely
attractive. Max began to invent new twists to the game. It is
reported that he and Tevendale would toss a coin to determine
who was to sleep with Sheila. Naturally Max was not willing to
be left out of the game, even when he lost. On those occasions,
he would insist that all three of them went to bed.

In his usual style, Max quickly became bored of Trudy and
Brian, and urged Sheila to move on so they could find new
partners. Sheila refused. Max then realised that she had fallen
in love with Tevendale. He was horrified. While happy for his

wife to sleep with Tevendale, falling in love was out of the question; he then devoted his time to attempting to split them up. Things began to unravel quickly, with Garvie threatening to incarcerate Sheila in a London clinic. There were many dramatic scenes, but Sheila did not stop seeing Tevendale. She sought help and advice from many quarters on how to end the marriage, but was urged to stay with her husband for the sake of the children.

On 14 May 1968, Max Garvie was witnessed driving to a meeting in Stonehaven. This was the last time he was seen alive. That night, Sheila seemed unusually anxious. Her eldest daughter reported that their mother had sent the three children to bed early that night, recalling that her mother seemed agitated. She had been drinking heavily all evening, and on bidding her children good night, she insisted, 'No matter what, don't get up.' The children slept, with no idea of the events that were to play out that night.

Exactly what happened in the early hours of the morning was hotly disputed by the various parties involved. Allegedly, Sheila Garvie admitted two men to the family home. This was disputed in court, with Tevendale saying they had not been to the house until Sheila called for help, while Sheila stated that they had let themselves in and killed Max without her involvement. Whatever the precise circumstances, two men entered the property, one being Tevendale, the other a friend of his, Alan Peters.

According to Peters's testimony, he had been told some weeks before that Tevendale wished to 'get rid of' someone, and had been asked to help with transport. Peters claimed to be present but not involved in the murder, and said that Sheila let both men in. Sheila was said to have guided the men upstairs and into the master bedroom, where Max lay fast asleep. Sheila had apparently made love to him earlier that evening, possibly to ensure his deep sleep. Tevendale did not waste time, and

knocked Garvie unconscious with one of his own rifles. While
Max lay unconscious and Sheila stood guard at the bedroom
doorway, Tevendale proceeded to shoot him in the head,
muffling the sound of the gun with a pillow.

The children slept through the noise. The adults, with their
nerves in shreds, went back downstairs and consumed a bottle
of whisky between them. Once they had calmed down, the
men returned upstairs where they wrapped Max's body in a
blanket and, in the dead of night, deposited it in Peters's car
boot. From there, they drove to Lauriston Castle, where
they dumped his body in a culvert which ran from Lauriston
Quarry to the castle.

The next day, Sheila reported Max as missing, claiming that
she bade him farewell the previous morning as he departed
for his meeting. He had not arrived home by the time she
retired to bed, and the next day, she had woken to find him
missing. A missing person report was issued, in which Garvie
was described as follows:

> Spends freely, is a heavy drinker and often consumes tran-
> quillisers when drinking. Is fond of female company . . . deals
> in pornographic material and is an active member of nudist
> camps . . . may have gone abroad.

He might well have remained missing indefinitely, had Sheila
not confided in her mother, Edith Watson, in early August,
stating that she believed that her boyfriend, Tevendale, 'might'
have murdered her husband. Edith, being a law-abiding sort and
disapproving of her daughter's relationship with Tevendale,
agonised over the situation for some days, before eventually
going to the police on 14 August. It is not clear why Sheila
revealed this information to her mother; it seems fairly certain
that she did not know where the body had been disposed of.
Perhaps she believed that she could pre-empt suspicion falling
upon her in the event that the body was discovered by having
implicated Tevendale early on. It is unlikely we will ever know,

as Sheila Garvie has remained tight-lipped on this aspect of her story ever since.

Garvie and Tevendale were arrested that day, Peters some time after. On 17 August 1968, Tevendale took the police to where Garvie's decomposing body was hidden.

The trial came to the High Court in Aberdeen on 19 November 1968, and provoked a media frenzy. Church groups were especially vocal, claiming that sinning leads only to destruction. All three defendants pleaded 'Not Guilty'. The court was packed, and the jury, along with benches full of members of the public, heard the full story of the Garvies' lifestyle. The court heard tales of 'perverts' tossing coins to determine their sexual partner for the night, and stories of the bizarre sexual practices that Max Garvie inflicted on Sheila, including the insistence she sleep with a man over a decade her junior. The judge declared it sordid, but the public were hooked. As the trial progressed, people queued for courtroom seats, arriving at the courthouse from 3.30 a.m. onwards.

As the trial progressed, both defendants denied responsibility for the killing, though Tevendale did not implicate Sheila beyond telling a tale of an extraordinary accident. Tevendale did not give evidence on his own behalf. His defence counsel claimed that he had received a phone call from Sheila in the middle of the night. Apparently, Sheila, in a terrible state, had told Tevendale that she had accidentally murdered her husband. The story went that Max Garvie had asked her to do 'something unnatural' with a rifle. When Sheila refused, a struggle ensued and the rifle went off, accidentally killing Max when a bullet hit him in the back of the head. Tevendale claimed that he and Alan Peters had hidden the body in a panic.

Sheila claimed that she awoke in the middle of the night to hear someone whispering her name – Tevendale. It was then she discovered that Tevendale and his friend Peters had murdered Max. The Crown's case stated that Sheila had enticed

Tevendale to murder her husband, and that they were equally to blame, having plotted the murder together in order to pursue their relationship without Garvie's interference.

The jury ruled unanimously that Tevendale was guilty. Sheila Garvie was found guilty, by a majority. Alan Peters was set free, as the jury did not consider that there was sufficient evidence to convict him, despite his admission that he was present when the murder took place. Both Brian Tevendale and Sheila Garvie were sentenced to life in prison.

During the trial, Tevendale and Sheila Garvie had claimed to be in love, and confirmed that they would be seeking permission to marry while in prison. However, three months into her sentence, Sheila wrote to Tevendale to state, 'I have decided to have nothing to do with you ever again.' The romance that prompted a murder had cooled rapidly, and they never saw each other again. Both were released in 1978. Tevendale married and led a quiet existence as a pub landlord in Perthshire. He died of a heart attack in 2003. Sheila Garvie married twice more. She has consistently maintained that her version of events is the truth.

BIBLE JOHN

Date: 1968-9
Place: Glasgow

The Barrowlands Dance Hall, more commonly known just as the Barrowlands, was one of Glasgow's most popular night-spots from when it first opened its doors in 1934. Over time, it has suffered from the vagaries of fashion, and now it is known as a major concert venue. But in the late 1960s, when dancing was all the rage, it was the place to go for the young men and women of the city. However, it was about to become famous for a completely different reason. In the space of less than two years, three women were murdered, and it was believed that all three met their killer at the Barrowlands. The newspapers thought the murders to be the work of one man: the serial killer they dubbed 'Bible John'.

Thursday nights at the Barrowlands were always well att-ended, because Thursday was 'Over-25s Night'. Not just a popular choice for singles of a certain age, it tended to be a night where married women took off their wedding rings and danced with married men seeking similar anonymity. A good many men calling themselves 'John' for the evening gravitated towards the Barrowlands, and illicit encounters were not uncommon.

On one such Thursday, 22 February 1968, Patricia Docker went to the Barrowlands. Patricia was married, though separ-ated from her husband, and she lived with her parents. A single mother, she worked hard at her job as an auxiliary nurse and was looking forward to a night off. Her parents had offered to babysit her four-year-old son, and she was ready for a night out dancing with her girlfriends. Patricia is believed to have attended another club, The Majestic, first, before moving on to the Barrowlands. She was quite an attractive woman, but not striking enough to stand out in the Barrowlands crowd that night, and there were no witnesses able to confirm her movements in any detail. Some people remembered seeing her in both the Majestic and the Barrowlands, but their recollections were sketchy and there was little information on any of her dance partners. Some witnesses vaguely recalled her leaving the Barrowlands with a gentleman who was to escort her home. This is the last time Patricia was seen alive.

Early the next morning, a local man was on his way to work. His route took him along a quiet lane, and as he walked he noticed something strange lying off to the side of the path. He went to investigate and was horrified to discover the dead, naked body of a young woman. He ran back to town to alert the police, who rushed to the scene. It was clear that the woman had been murdered: the killer had battered her, then strangled her with her own stockings and tossed her body to the side of the lane. Besides the stockings, there were no other items around the body and no sign of her handbag or other clothing. The police began to consider the possibility that she had been murdered elsewhere and her body dumped in the lane.

Patricia's parents were aware that their daughter had not arrived home, but assumed she had stayed overnight with a friend, only to hear of the discovery of a body, which they confirmed later to be that of their missing daughter. The police scoured the local area for her clothes and handbag, and sent divers into the local river. Nothing was ever found. Desperate for clues, police circulated photos of Patricia, along with a description of her clothing, in the hope that some of the local people might have seen her after her departure from the dancehall. But no new leads came to light, and the case remained unsolved.

Eighteen months passed, and Patricia Docker's murder had been largely forgotten. Women who had feared for their safety relaxed their guard and the Barrowlands remained as popular as ever. On Saturday 16 August 1969, single mother Jemima McDonald left her three children with her sister Margaret, and headed into Glasgow for a night of dancing at the Barrowlands. She often went there on a Thursday night, so it is possible that she had caught the eye of a man, or even danced with him, on a previous evening. Her friends did not remember a great deal of detail about the evening. They reported seeing Jemima dancing most of the evening with 'a tall fair-haired man, in a light blue suit'. The pair left the dance hall together towards the end of the night. Like Patricia, this was the last sighting of Jemima, until her body was discovered the next day in a disused building close to where she lived. She, like Patricia, had been strangled with her own stockings.

If this created a sense of unease in the women of Glasgow, it developed into full-blown hysteria when the body of 29-year-old Helen Puttock was discovered not two months later. Helen had been out to the Barrowlands with her sister Jean on Thursday 30 October 1969. The case differed from the previous two as Helen's sister, Jean Puttock, witnessed a number of exchanges between a man named John and her sister, and even shared a taxi home with them. The two sisters had spent the evening in the company of two gentlemen, both calling themselves John. As the evening drew to a close, the two couples left for home. Jean's partner (known for convenience as 'Castlemilk John' as he claimed to live in Castlemilk) left the group to get a bus home. Helen, Jean and the second John shared a taxi. Jean got out at Earltown and went home. The taxi continued across town to Scotstoun where Helen lived. However, Helen never made it home.

A local man walking his dog found her body the next morning. She, too, had been strangled and her handbag was missing.

The crime scene differed from the previous cases, in that her killer had left not only a bite mark, but also semen on her clothes. This evidence, coupled with a good physical description and a detailed statement from Jean, finally gave police a starting-point for their investigation. After three murders, police believed they might at last have a lead.

A strange aspect of the Bible John murders was that each victim had been menstruating at the time of her death. This may have been coincidence, but for a while police explored the possibility that the killer may have viewed menstruating women as dirty. He was heard to utter a number of phrases in Jean's presence that implied familiarity with the bible, and he was quoted by Jean as saying, 'I don't drink at Hogmanay. I pray.' From this, it was not a great stretch of the imagination to consider that the killer had beliefs in accordance with 'Mosaic Law' (Leviticus 15.19) and considered a menstruating woman to be 'unclean'. The police explored the possibility that he had previously entertained women without incident, but in the case of his three victims had become angry and violent when he discovered their condition. His first two victims had been strangled, but there was no evidence of sexual assault. However, police investigations failed to turn up any reports of women who had been entertained by a man meeting 'John's' description, and had escaped unharmed, and the theory remained an intriguing but unproved possibility.

The Barrowlands was always sweaty, smoky and packed. It was a place where women would go to let their hair down and hitch their skirts up, and dance with men who were simply seeking a bit of fun. Combined with a steady flow of alcohol, it was not surprising that few people noticed what was going on around them. But Helen's sister was able to give a far more detailed description of the prime suspect than the previous vague accounts from witnesses. He was described as being around 6' 1", with sandy-coloured fair hair, and slightly overlapping front teeth. Police circulated an artist's impression of the suspect in the hope that further witnesses might come forward.

Jean Puttock's memory of the numerous bible quotes he had been heard to utter over the course of the evening prompted police and the media to dub him 'Bible John'. Jean provided the police with as much information as she could remember, and willingly attended over three hundred identification parades. One person who never resurfaced was Jean's dancing partner on that evening, 'Castlemilk John'. Jean had danced with him throughout the evening, and had suspected that he may have been married, though he never confirmed or denied this. The sisters and their respective partners had formed a foursome and spent time drinking and dancing together over the course of the evening, giving the men plenty of time for conversation.

'Castlemilk John' told Jean that he was a builder and lived in Castlemilk. The charitable viewpoint might be that he read the newspaper reports, and felt that he had nothing further to add that could help the case. It is equally likely that, if married, he may have decided that he did not wish to complicate his life by letting his wife know that he had danced the night away at the Barrowlands.

Bible John gave away some details about himself to Helen, which she shared with her sister while they were in the cloak-room; something about where he lived or worked, but Jean had been unable to remember this. Desperate to retrieve any detail which might help to find her sister's killer, Jean was prepared to undergo hypnosis to try and retrieve the lost memory, but this was vetoed by the Edinburgh Crown Office.

Jean did remember watching a strange exchange between her sister and Bible John during the evening, which took place by a cigarette machine in the Barrowlands. John appeared to be telling Helen something, which she seemed to disbelieve, laughing and looking incredulous. Bible John then pulled a small card from his pocket and showed it to her, and immediately the expression on her face settled to one of acceptance. Jean tried to see the card, but John quickly concealed it, telling her, 'You know what happens to nosy people.' It is not known what was on the card, but it clearly prompted a change in attitude from Helen.

A major investigation was under way in Glasgow, led by Detective Superintendent Joe Beattie. Initially detectives were hopeful: Jean's description was highly detailed, and had provided the police with a number of promising starting points. From the bite mark on the body it was apparent that the murderer's front teeth not only overlapped, but he was missing a tooth in his upper right jaw. Police set up a massive task force and interviewed hundreds of Glasgow dentists.

The investigation yielded over five thousand potential suspects. All were interviewed and eliminated, and the dental lead petered out, despite the fact that the tooth extraction was likely to have been carried out by a dentist; perhaps the killer had not visited a dentist for a number of years, or a dentist in another part of the country had carried out the extraction.

Bible John had a distinctive hair colour and a rather unfashionable style – red or sandy, and cut fairly short and rounded at the back. Police questioned a number of local hairdressers and barbers, but again to no avail. The police considered briefly whether the killer had been wearing some kind of false hair, but the theory was eliminated, as it was unlikely that Jean would have missed this after spending so long in his company. The public latched on to the fact that Bible John was known to have short red hair, and innocent men with a similar hairstyle or colouring were persecuted to the point that it became necessary for the Glasgow police to issue official cards bearing the phrase, 'I am not Bible John'. Business at the Barrowlands fell dramatically, with the vast majority of the clientèle being undercover police officers hoping to catch a glimpse of their quarry. Bible John, however, seemed to disappear into thin air. He has never been caught.

*　*　*

Although the trail went cold, the story has remained in the public consciousness, and resurfaces in newspapers at regular intervals. In 1996, it seemed the case might be solved when Strathclyde Police announced that they were going to exhume the body of John McInnes, to compare his DNA with that of the semen taken from Helen Puttock's clothes. McInnes had committed suicide in 1981, at the age of 41, and the police were confident enough of the outcome that they stated they were all but certain he was the killer. Five months later, they were forced to admit that the DNA evidence did not confirm their suspicions.

Detective Superintendent Beattie, who led the original investigation, died in 2000, but was quoted as saying, 'No one ever really thought one man had killed three times. The cases were never really linked.'

In 2005, the Strathclyde Police carried out a 'cold case' review, and concluded that the serial killer 'Bible John' was a media invention, and did not actually exist.

In 2008, the possibility of Peter Tobin, a convicted killer of three women, being Bible John was suggested. Tobin is reported to have told a prison psychiatrist that he had killed forty-eight women, before smiling and saying, 'Prove it.' Extensive research has been carried out as to the possible link by a leading criminologist, Professor David Wilson, who stated that he would stake his credibility on Bible John being Peter Tobin. Wilson had spent three years investigating Tobin, and initially had not set out to link Tobin to Bible John.

However, while watching Tobin's trial, he had a revelation. Listening to the testimony of a witness who had accompanied

Dinah McNicol in a taxi driven by Tobin shortly before her death, the witness reported the conversation between Tobin and McNicol. Tobin was discussing the Liphook Music Festival with her, saying that his taste leaned towards the Cambridge Folk Festival. Wilson, hearing this testimony, immediately drew links to the Bible John case, where the killer shared a taxi with Helen Puttock. Her sister Jean reported that Bible John had been keen to imply that he was socially superior, in this case by claiming not to support a football team or drink at Hogmanay. For a young man purportedly living in Glasgow in the sixties, this was unusual.

The Barrowlands murders stopped abruptly, leading police to suspect that the killer had left the area. Tobin could have exaggerated the number of women he killed for dramatic effect, but in reality it is possible that he did kill this number over an extended period of time. Serial killers sometimes murder in one part of the country, and then move to another part. Unless the *modus operandi* is extremely similar, it can be difficult to link murders being investigated by a number of police forces. Certainly, Tobin's movements over the years do seem to match a considerable number of unsolved murders in the corresponding parts of the country, and it seems reasonable to assume that he was responsible for at least some.

There are further similarities between Bible John and Tobin. Tobin often used aliases, one of these being John Semple. Jean reported that her sister's killer had called himself either John 'Sempleson' or 'Templeson'. Tobin lived in Glasgow at the time of the Barrowlands murders, which stopped around the same time as he moved on. There are differences, which Wilson believes can be explained. Tobin is only 5' 8", whereas the descriptions of Bible John tended to place him at around 6 feet. Wilson has extensively examined the statements, and has noted that Bible John seemed to increase in height each time Jean Puttock was interviewed, so he may not have been as tall as police thought. The DNA evidence recovered from Helen's body would have proven conclusively either way, but it has transpired that the DNA was stored in such a way that it is no longer viable for testing.

In June 2010, a Glasgow grandmother contacted the newspapers after seeing a photograph of Tobin as a young man, and identified him as the man with whom she had a terrifying encounter in the Barrowlands in the late 1960s. In September 2010, Jean Puttock, the only person likely to be able to identify Bible John, passed away.

The circumstantial evidence is persuasive, but the truth is, after all this time, and barring a confession from the killer, it is unlikely that conclusive proof will ever be found to establish the true identity of Bible John.

THE BUTLER DID IT

Date: 1977
Place: Dumfriesshire

Born in 1895, Captain Walter Travers Scott-Elliot had a long
and distinguished career, firstly as a serving officer in the First
World War, then in business as the managing director of East
India Merchants. He entered public service, serving in the
Ministry of Labour during the Second World War before
becoming a Labour MP in 1945, but did not contest his seat
in the 1950 election, returning to business until his retirement
in the late 1960s. His business dealing had amassed him a
considerable fortune, including a fine selection of antiques and
Indian jewellery. In addition to the family estates in Dumfriesshire, he and his Indian-born wife, Dorothy, had homes in
Knightsbridge, Nice and Rome.

In November 1977, the Scott-Elliots were looking for a new
butler for their Knightsbridge flat. Roy Fontaine appeared to
be an ideal choice; with his polished manners, and smooth
unruffled demeanour, he seemed everything a good butler
should be. He was given the job. Little did the Scott-Elliots
know that they had hired a man who had been convicted of
jewel theft, and three months before had murdered a man in
cold blood. It was a mistake that would cost them their lives.

Born on 17 June 1924 in McLean Street, Partick, Archibald
Thomson Hall was raised in the tenements of Glasgow. The
poverty of his upbringing and a disinclination to do a hard
day's work led Hall to commence a life of crime at the tender
age of fifteen. While showing an appetite for breaking the law
on a regular basis, he showed no similar talent for evading

detection, and a string of offences saw him behind bars for the first time at the age of seventeen, for theft. On his release he got his first taste for the good things in life when he was seduced by a wealthy older woman, who would take him for meals at expensive hotels, and who introduced him to life at the higher end of society. In fact, Hall was bisexual, and later in life he had a short-lived marriage that broke up when his proclivities became more apparent.

Another conviction followed at the age of nineteen – this time for burglary – and another in 1944. Still craving to climb the social ladder, Hall decided to head for the Mecca of high society: London. He was an avid film-goer, and decided that he needed a glamorous new name to match his new surroundings. He adopted the surname of the star of Hitchcock's *Rebecca*: plain Archibald Hall had become the debonair Roy Fontaine. Charming and handsome, 'Fontaine' made an impression on the social scene, and is rumoured to have had sexual encounters with Lord Boothby and playwright Terence Rattigan. To support his new lifestyle, his life of crime continued, with predictable results. A charge of forgery led to another two years.

Over the years, Hall had developed the ability to pass himself off as someone of breeding and charm, able to mix comfortably with members of high society; he added this to his repertoire of crime in 1952, gaining a job as a butler with a wealthy Stirlingshire family. When they were away on holiday, he hired a suit, borrowed the family Bentley, and attended a reception at Holyrood Palace in their stead, robbing an antique shop on the way home. On another occasion he posed as an Arab prince, using the subterfuge to invite some jewellers to his suite at a top London hotel, and escaping with a haul of jewellery as a result.

Caught by the police once more, in 1956 he was sentenced to a total of thirty years and sent to Parkhurst. Moved to a prison near Lowestoft in the mid-sixties, he escaped and was recaptured, receiving an additional five years for his pains. By the time he eventually emerged from prison, yet again, in 1975, constant practice had eradicated any trace of his Glaswegian accent. Well-versed in social etiquette, he had also acquired a comprehensive knowledge of antiques. Well-prepared, he set off once more to find work as a butler, determined that his life of petty crime should be at an end; he was in search of richer rewards.

He was able to secure a post with Lady Margaret Hudson, at Kirtleton House in Dumfriesshire. She was the 77-year-old widow of a Tory M. P., and her house was full of valuable antiques. Hall had fallen into a relationship with a prostitute named Mary Coggle, known better as Belfast Mary. Hall maintained to his friends that he was now going straight, not wishing to reveal his designs on Lady Hudson's antiques; he was just biding his time.

Hall's carefully laid plans were thrown into disarray when a former cell-mate and ex-lover, David Wright, arrived at Kirtleton House. Wright was looking for work, and used his knowledge of Hall's past, and the threat of exposure, to persuade the butler to find him a job in Lady Hudson's employ. Hall passed Wright off as his nephew, and as a result, Wright was given accommodation and some work as a gamekeeper and gardener. After Wright had spent three weeks keeping down the rabbit population, Hall discovered that he had stolen a silver tray and a valuable ring from Lady Hudson; Hall was incensed, and tracked down the stolen items, returning the ring to Lady Hudson's jewellery box. Hall maintained he was now going straight, but in reality, Wright was disrupting Hall's own long-term felonious schemes. Wright sought to teach Hall a lesson; waiting until Lady Hudson was away, and after consuming considerable amounts of her Ladyship's champagne, he fired a shot into the headboard of Hall's bed as he slept, and hit him in the face with the rifle butt before Hall was able calm him down with a promise to join him in a scheme to steal a substantial number of valuables from the house. Clearly, Hall had to deal with the situation, which was beginning to get out of control.

The following day, Hall suggested the two of them go out shooting in the woods to talk things over. Hall's life of crime to that day had been singularly free of violence, but that was about to change dramatically. Waiting until Wright had used his ammunition Hall stepped behind him, and shot him in the back of the head. He concealed Wright's body in a shallow grave in Pokeskinesike Burn, about half a mile from the house; later he returned to it several times to improve its concealment.

However, something of Hall's history did reach the ears of Lady Hudson, and Hall was soon looking for work once more. Three months after the murder of David Wright, Roy Fontaine, alias Archie Hall, took up his new position in the Knightsbridge flat of Walter Scott-Elliot, with its array of priceless antiques. As Hall settled into his role as the perfect butler, he found that the Scott-Elliots were in need of a cleaner, and who better to fill the role than his prostitute friend, Mary Coggle, who was soon busy dusting the priceless ornaments in the flat.

It was through Mary Coggle that Hall met Michael Kitto in a London pub. Kitto was a thirty-nine-year-old petty thief, who was on the run from the police after stealing £1000 from the pub where he was working. They became friends, and started to discuss the criminal possibilities offered by Hall's trusted position as the Scott-Elliots' butler. They envisaged a plan which would enable Kitto to burgle the flat, but leave Hall still in place and unsuspected, to plan further schemes. On the night of 8 December 1977, Hall let Kitto into the flat to show him around. The elderly Scott-Elliot had retired to bed with his customary dose of sleeping-pills, and Hall believed the sixty-year-old Dorothy Scott-Elliot was away staying in a nursing home, leaving the two of them to plan the burglary without fear of interruption. Unfortunately for Mrs Scott-Elliot, she was at home, and when she surprised the pair of them, she guessed that something was going on. Before she could cry for help, Hall threw her to the floor, and while Kitto held her down, he held a pillow over her face until she stopped struggling. They had hardly put her body in her bed, and hastily covered her, when they heard Walter Scott-Elliot coming. Hall was able to convince him that the noise he had heard was his wife having a nightmare, but that all was well; the old man, still drowsy from his sleeping-pills, returned to bed.

Hastily formulating a plan, Hall waited until Scott-Elliot went out the following morning, then enlisted the help of Mary Coggle. She was to pose as the late Mrs Scott-Elliot, and in this guise accepted delivery of a hired car. When Scott-Elliot returned, Hall drugged him with his own sleeping-pills, loaded his wife's body into the boot of the car, and Hall, Kitto, the old man and Mary Coggle (still dressed as his wife) set off in the car together. They stopped for the night in a rented cottage outside Carlisle, and continued on into Scotland the following day, stopping to throw the body of Dorothy Scott-Elliot into a ditch.

That night they stayed at a hotel in Blair Atholl, before continuing on to Invernesshire. Depositing the still-drugged Scott-Elliot in a hotel with Mary Coggle, still posing as his wife, Hall and Kitto returned to London to sell some of the items they had stolen from the flat. Returning to Scotland, Hall had to decide what to do with the elderly ex-M.P. Driving to one of the loneliest glens in the area, Hall and Kitto took him into the trees, and attempted to strangle him. The old man put up a surprisingly vigorous struggle, and they were obliged to finish him off with the shovel they had brought to dig his grave. They hid his body in a clump of rhododendrons; Mary Coggle had waited in the car while this went on.

They made their way back to Edinburgh to decide their next move. Mary Coggle wanted to go back to London, but also wanted to keep the expensive mink coat and jewellery that had been her disguise for the last few days. Hall was totally against the idea; she could hardly fail to attract attention with her new-found wealth, but Coggle was insistent: another problem for Hall to solve. They returned to the rented cottage, where the quarrel arose again; Hall hit her over the head with a poker, and with Kitto's help, overpowered and suffocated her. They then went down to the pub to plan their next move. The following day they dumped her body, and headed back to London for Christmas.

Returning to the Scott-Elliots' flat for the final time, Hall and Kitto cleared it of all the antiques, jewellery and cash. It was at this stage that a new face appeared on the scene. Donald was Archibald Hall's younger brother; he was a petty thief, with none of his brother's charm or intelligence, and he had just been released from Perth Prison after serving a sentence for assaulting young girls. Tagging along with Hall and Kitto, even his dull wits could hardly fail to notice that they were unusually flush with cash. His brother's constant questions becoming an irritation to him, Hall realised he had yet another problem to solve. They were staying once more in the rented cottage near Carlisle, when Donald decided to show them a useful skill he had acquired: the ability to tie someone up using only six inches of string. It proved to be a fatal mistake.

Donald lay on the floor, and instructed the others to tie his thumbs together behind his back. Then he told them to push his feet between his wrists, thus immobilising him. Hall was not one to pass up a chance like this. With the help of Kitto, he thrust a cloth impregnated with chloroform over his brother's mouth, and after a fierce struggle, Donald Hall lapsed into unconsciousness. Hall and Kitto carried him to the bathroom, and drowned him in the bath.

Stashing the body in the boot of the car, together with a spade, the pair of them headed back to Scotland again, with another impromptu burial on their agenda; but they had reckoned without the extremes of a Scottish winter. They were caught in a blizzard, and when they finally reached the preferred spot for the interment, they found they could make no impression on the frozen ground with their spade. Cutting their losses for the day, they drove into North Berwick, and booked a room for the night at the Blenheim House Hotel in the name of Ponton.

The manager of the hotel was Norman Wight, and there was something about the two men that aroused his suspicion. His first thought, as they ordered rounds of drinks to be put on their bill, was that they were going to dine there, then slip off early in the morning without paying the bill. Kitto remained mostly silent, but Hall was being voluble, telling a story about how he was taking a final tour of Britain before emigrating. As Hall and Kitto sat down to their dinner, Norman Wight decided to take the prudent step of phoning the police.

A young police constable arrived in a police car, and ran a check on the car that Hall had left in the hotel car park. This soon established that the number-plate did not match the car it was attached to, and the tax disc was a forgery. This was more than enough for Hall and Kitto to be transported to the local station, while Mr Wight, at the police's request, searched their room. He found an envelope containing 76 silver Edwardian coins. While he was doing this, a police officer was searching the car, and on opening the boot, discovered the body of Donald Hall.

On their arrival at the police station, Kitto lost no time in admitting everything, while Hall lost no time in escaping.

After asking to go to the toilet, he wriggled out of the window, leaving a pound note behind on the cistern. He was travelling in a taxi along the A1 when he was finally detained at a police road-block. In the meantime, Kitto had been giving a detailed account of the murders, and a rough description of where the bodies were buried. Mary Coggle's body had been found already, but had remained unidentified, but it took some days, and the efforts of several hundred officers, before the bodies of Mr and Mrs Scott-Elliot were found. Realising that there was little point in concealing the facts, Hall advised them where to find David Wright, someone the police did not even know was missing.

With the death penalty abolished, Hall realised the length of the sentence that awaited him, and attempted suicide with tranquillisers that he had managed to conceal from the police, but he failed, and after examination, was declared sane and fit to plead. The Scottish trial covered only the murders that took place on Scottish soil. Hall and Kitto pleaded guilty; Hall was sentenced to serve a minimum of fifteen years. In the subsequent trial at the Old Bailey, Hall was given another life sentence, and Kitto a minimum of fifteen years. The Old Bailey judge recommended that Hall should never be released, and he never was. He made numerous suicide attempts that failed, and published an autobiography, *A Perfect Gentleman*, in 1999. He died of a stroke in Kingston Prison, Portsmouth, in 2002, at the age of 78.